UNDERCOVER WASHINGTON

For Ron and Mike

TOURING THE SITES
WHERE FAMOUS SPIES LIVED, WORKED AND LOVED

UNDERCOVER
WASHINGTON

PAMELA KESSLER

EPM
PUBLICATIONS, INC./McLEAN, VIRGINIA

Library of Congress Cataloging-in-Publication Data

Kessler, Pamela.
    Undercover Washington : touring the sites where famous spies
lived, worked, and loved / Pamela Kessler.
        p.   cm.
    Includes bibliographical references and index.
    ISBN 0-939009-60-9
    1. Historic sites—Washington Region—Guidebooks.   2. Espionage—
Washington Region—History.   3. Washington Region—Guidebooks.
I. Title.
F195.K47   1992
917.5304′4—dc20   91-47883
                                                                        CIP

EPM Publications, Inc., 1003 Turkey Run Road
    McLean, VA 22101
Printed in the United States of America

Cover and book design by Tom Huestis
Maps by Kimberley Roll

CONTENTS

ACKNOWLEDGMENTS

FOR MAKING THIS BOOK POSSIBLE, THANKS:
to **Ronald Kessler**, *my husband, who allowed me to pick his brain at will, day and night. His generosity is exceeded only by his patience. For their enthusiastic support, I thank my son,* **Mike Whitehead**, *who teaches me about writing through his music; my stepchildren,* **Greg V. Kessler** *and* **Rachel Kessler**; *and my parents,* **Frederick** *and* **Edith Johnson**. *Thanks too to* **Evelyn P. Metzger** *for her thoughtful encouragement.*

I'd be remiss if I didn't mention at least a few of the helpful guides I've been lucky enough to meet on the way to putting this book together. My special thanks to **John E. Taylor** *at the National Archives, and to* **Edwin C. Fishel** *for setting me straight on the Civil War, as well as to:* **Elizabeth Bancroft, Russell J. Bowen, Bill Deary, E. Peter Earnest, Alan Hall, Edward Hawkins, Sam Halpern, John L. Martin, Linda McCarthy, Michael P. Musick, Eda Offutt, Hayden Peake,** *and* **Sandra Weber**.

This is a tour that no one can confirm or deny. It's a walk through what former CIA counterintelligence chief James Jesus Angleton called "a wilderness of mirrors"—in Washington, D.C., the spy capital of the world.

The original American spymaster, George Washington, had his home just across the river at Mount Vernon. During the Civil War, the city—strategically located between Confederate Virginia and Secessionist-leaning Maryland—was a hotbed of espionage activity. In fact, in every major war, including the Cold War, the capital has been the target—not for a repeat of the War of 1812, when the British set fire to it, but for something subtler, done with smoke and mirrors. In peacetime, the capital continues to engage in intelligence gathering. The government agencies, the allies, the current perceived enemy—everybody does it.

Major advances in cryptology happened here—the breaking of the Japanese Purple cipher, and ones we never hear about because the National Security Agency keeps them top secret. Major figures in espionage history like Kim Philby and "Wild Bill" Donovan lived and worked here, and some, like John Walker, had their drop sites here. It's the home of the CIA, the FBI and the Pentagon—the principal targets of respectable spies.

There's only one plaque on this tour and only one souvenir shop. Anyone who visits the spy sites of Washington should be forewarned: You won't see a lot. The nature of the game is to remain hidden. The players don't want to be observed. They leave no traces. If you want neon signs and topless dancers jumping into fountains, take the scandal tour.

If, on the other hand, you appreciate the covert art of dead drops, brush contacts, decrypts and disinformation, then grab an empty 7-Up can, and read on.

1. La Niçoise
   1721 Wisconsin Avenue
2. Dumbarton Oaks
   31st and R Streets
3. Site of Georgetown Pharmacy
   1344 Wisconsin Avenue

   Alger Hiss Homes
4. 2905 P Street
5. 1245 30th Street
6. 3415 Volta Place
7. Russell J. Bowen Collection
   Lauinger Library
   Georgetown University
   37th and Prospect Streets
8. Au Pied de Cochon
   1335 Wisconsin Avenue
9. Former Soviet Embassy Buildings
   2650 Wisconsin Avenue
10. Home of "Wild Bill" Donovan
    2920 R Street

A Wilderness of Mirrors
La Niçoise
1721 Wisconsin Avenue N.W.

For two decades, James Jesus Angleton was the CIA's powerful chief of counterintelligence. He called the world of espionage "a wilderness of mirrors." The personification of a "clandestine mentality," he claimed that moles had burrowed into the agency; he struck fear in the hearts of its employees and ruined some of their careers. He saw double agents in spies recruited by the CIA in communist countries and defectors as messengers of disinformation. He was forced to retire in 1974 by then-director William Colby. "His ultraconspiratorial turn of mind had. . .become more of a liability than an asset to the agency," Colby said.

Angleton was gaunt, but a big eater. When he frequented La Niçoise, a small French restaurant in upper Georgetown, Michel Bigotti used to wait on him. Bigotti, now the restaurant's manager, smiled to himself at the mention of Angleton.

"Ah, the King of Spies," he said. "He came the first day we opened." That was in 1969. "Table 41, always the same table, always with a reservation." For years he ate there almost every day, around 12:30. The table was in the back, in front of the mirror. It was the perfect poker-player's seat with a view of the room and the front door.

Angleton would start with an I.W. Harper bourbon, "not too many cubes," according to Bigotti. "Raw oysters or clams as an appetizer, then a lot of seafood—shad and shad roe, scampi. Or calf's liver. No dessert. Once in a while he was drinking Kir, but mostly bourbon, two of them," Bigotti said. He tipped precisely 15 percent and chain-smoked Virginia Slims.

Except for strewing cigarette ashes about himself, he was a fastidious man who favored handcrafted fly-fishing lures, the poetry of T.S. Eliot and his own homegrown orchids—especially the lady-

11

slipper. Why did such an aesthete dine regularly at a restaurant with a rowdy floor show and waiters on rollerskates?

"He was coming here I think because it wasn't a serious place," Bigotti recalled. "At the time there were not so many French restaurants. People used to come from Capitol Hill for lunch."

Besides, Bigotti said, "They don't skate for lunch. Only at night. He didn't look like a spy to me. He didn't look dangerous. But everybody knew here he was a spy."

In fact, once in anticipation of Angleton's lunch, the waiters arranged a stage microphone among the flowers on Table 41. According to Christian Renault, who was the chef, when Angleton was shown to the table with a friend from the French embassy, he said sternly, "Would you take this away please?" But he kept coming back to the restaurant.

"He had his little peculiarities," Renault recalled. When he ordered mussels, he wanted them very large, and only those with orange-colored flesh. Renault never knew why. "Of course," he said, "you only know the color of the mussel when it opens." So before sending them to the table, the chef dutifully removed any white ones.

Angleton was not always so discriminating in choosing lunch partners. One of his lunch buddies had been Soviet superspy Harold "Kim" Philby at the time when he was a mole in the British Embassy. Angleton, the legendary spy catcher, had had no idea.

After his retirement and fall from grace, he adopted the Army and Navy Club at 17th and Eye Streets N.W. as the locus for his lunches. The bourbons were a thing of the past. After he came under public scrutiny in 1974—at one point his lawn was covered with journalists—he quit drinking. He switched to Coke, no ice, with a slice of lemon. The biggest secret of all was that he never, on his own, caught a spy.

What's a Little Spying Among Friends?
Dumbarton Oaks
31st and R Streets N.W.

In summer, when the spring rush is over, the gardens of Dumbarton Oaks are lush, secret places. In the Orangerie, the clay-tile floor is cool and wet, and fig branches festoon the walls—the fig has been growing inside the room since before the Civil War. Out on the brick walks lined with boxwood, there are more chipmunks than people. Hot, sweet breath rises from the grass. Robins, when approached, flutter away at the last possible moment: It is their province here, among the trickling fountains, the urns and finials, the day-lilies, the rose parterres.

Or so it must have seemed that day in July 1984, when Jonathan Jay Pollard came here to meet his Israeli handler, Avi Sella. The two men walked behind the mansion, back to where the gardens start to blend into the woods, around Forsythia Hill. Pollard, a research specialist with the Naval Investigative Service in Suitland, Maryland, had brought classified documents with him, which he showed to Sella, an Israeli Air Force pilot. Pollard also showed him a satellite photo of an Iraqi nuclear reactor, taken shortly after an Israeli air strike that the pilot had commanded. Colonel Sella was neither pleased nor flattered. He was furious: It was one more bit of intelligence that the Americans weren't sharing with their allies.

That was what it was all about, and that's why Pollard, who was Jewish, was trying to help. But Sella didn't accept the documents on this encounter. First, he had some business to attend to. He had to compromise Pollard a little more: He talked money. In this regard, the universal clandestine philosophy was elegantly simple: Once you get a spy to accept money, he or she is yours. Soon Pollard and his wife were getting twice their net salaries from Israel.

Perhaps Pollard should have read the message spelled out in stones in the pebble pond: *Quod Severis Metes*—"As you sow, so shall you reap."

For it wasn't long before he was being suspected back at work. His area of expertise was terrorism in the U.S. and the Caribbean, and here he was, requesting volumes of information on the Middle East. His Israeli handlers presented him with detailed "tasking"—a shopping list. And Pollard went shopping—for strategic information about other Middle Eastern countries, for data on specific weapons systems, and for the Cartier diamond of the lot, a handbook on worldwide communications intelligence.

When the FBI came to talk to him in November 1985 about the documents he was borrowing, Pollard called his wife. Anne Pollard was at home in their apartment at 1733 20th Street N.W., a four-story building a block off Connecticut Avenue, waiting to go to meet Sella and his wife for dinner. Pollard told her to get rid of the "cactus." Anne Pollard, who knew most of what was going on, recognized the coded instruction to clean out any classified documents from their apartment. She gathered them into a suitcase and ran out to the back alley. Seeing several cars with their motors running, she rightly suspected the worst—FBI. She went back into the building and hid the documents under a staircase. Later, she per-

Pamela Kessler

Jonathan Pollard walked with his Israeli handler in the bosky glens of Dumbarton Oaks, which has as its motto "As you sow, so shall you reap."

14

suaded friends to pick up the suitcase for her, but instead of meeting with her to return it, they passed it to the FBI.

Two days later, Pollard called the Israeli embassy and was told that if he and his wife could lose the FBI tail, the Pollards could come in. At 3514 International Drive N.W., the brick building with windows like half moons is singularly forbidding, with its fences, security cameras and satellite dishes. The Pollards got as far as the driveway, thinking they had reached a life raft. But the FBI had surrounded the building. The embassy's chief security officer threw them back.

Anne Pollard got five years; Jonathan Pollard got life. At first, Colonel Sella was promoted to a fast-track new command in Israel. But after the U.S. indicted him, the Israelis had second thoughts and, for the sake of appearances, asked him to resign.

"Oh So Social"
Former home of "Wild Bill" Donovan
2920 R Street N.W.

In the early days of the CIA, Georgetown was an enclave for the agency. At times the spook population has been as dense as text in a microdot—of former directors and former station chiefs who headed CIA outposts at embassies. It was natural for OSS types (read moneyed Ivy-Leaguers) to gravitate to their proper places among Washington cave dwellers.

"Wild Bill" Donovan, founder of the Office of Strategic Services, was the paradigm. And he owned what was arguably the best house in the neighborhood, a stately brick residence facing historic Oak Hill Cemetery and overlooking Georgetown from the back. Set half a block back from the street, with gates leading to a circular drive, it is reminiscent of an English country house.

With the help of British intelligence experts including William S. Stephenson, the secret agent known as INTREPID, Donovan spent long hours here preparing a paper for FDR on the theory and practice of clandestine service. Donovan's 1941 report included the dictum that became the *raison d'être* for intelligence-gathering services around the world: "Strategy, without information on which it can rely, is helpless."

Because of his undercover war work, which included keeping FDR abreast of British intelligence on Hitler's actions, the president dubbed Donovan "my secret legs." In fact, his work was so secret that when he began holding confidential meetings in the Georgetown mansion, Donovan asked his wife to move out to their farm in Berryville, Virginia, for the duration. Everyone from statesmen to traitors crossed the portal of the Georgetown house, and most of them didn't want to be seen.

In June 1942, Donovan became the first director of the OSS. The Japanese surprise attack on Pearl Harbor seven months before had been an object lesson in the need for such an agency to coordinate intelligence.

As a World War I hero in France, Donovan had earned the nickname "Wild Bill." Now he picked up another: Within the British Secret Intelligence Service, he became formally known as "Q." The OSS earned a few sobriquets as well, mostly from columnist Drew Pearson: the "Cloak and Dagger Club," "Oh So Secret," and "Oh So Social."

Rendezvous at Georgetown Pharmacy
Site of Georgetown Pharmacy
1344 Wisconsin Avenue N.W.

Elizabeth Bentley was known as the "Red Spy Queen" when she testified in 1948 before the House Un-American Activities Committee. For the occasion, she wore a slinky black silk dress and pinned two artificial red roses in her light brown hair. A Vassar graduate, Bentley had been working on her masters at Columbia in 1935 when she became a member of the

Communist Party. She acted as a courier, carrying secret data to the Russians from communist sympathizers who worked in the U.S. government, from Agriculture to the OSS (Duncan Lee, director "Wild Bill" Donovan's confidential assistant). She also acquired material from columnist Walter Lippmann's files, supplied without his knowledge by his secretary, Mary Price.

In the early 1940s, every two weeks Bentley came to Washington to attend a cell meeting at the home of a couple who lived near Chevy Chase Circle. Sipping *chai* with her fellow revolutionaries, she handed out the latest communist literature. In return, she left with a briefcase stuffed with pilfered documents, which she took back to New York to her contact and lover, Yasha, and Soviet intelligence.

On one of her trips to Washington, she met her new Soviet control "Al" at the Georgetown Pharmacy. The FBI would later identify Al as Anatoliy Gromov, first secretary of the Soviet embassy and the top man in Soviet intelligence here. Though the drugstore closed down a few years ago, to be replaced by a women's clothing boutique, for decades it was a Washington landmark presided over by "Doc" Dalinsky.

Bentley had instructions to carry a copy of *Life Magazine*. She probably bought it there. Wearing a hat with a red flower for identification, Bentley waited on the corner for what seemed like hours. Finally Al showed up, with apologies for the incompetence of a subordinate who had delayed him. Al decided that he and Bentley would go to dinner at a seafood restaurant on the waterfront.

Al ran across Wisconsin Avenue through the heavy traffic and stopped a cab. But Bentley waited until traffic cleared, then crossed. When she got to the other side, Al glared at her."You have kept me waiting," he said frostily.

It was about this time that Bentley decided to give up the spy business.

As she noted in her biography, she had begun to see that the American Communist Party was just a tool of the KGB. In 1945, she supplied the FBI with the names of more than 25 U.S. government employees linked to the Soviet underground. Among them were Harry Dexter White, assistant secretary of the Treasury, and Alger Hiss, a rising young State Department official. This was not the first time Hiss's name would be raised; nor would it be the last.

Pumpkins and Perjury
Former homes of Alger Hiss at
2905 P Street N.W., 1245 30th Street N.W.,
and 3415 Volta Place N.W.

Alger Hiss was the central figure in the great spy hunt of the late 1940s. A lawyer and State Department employee, he was denounced by journalist and ex-communist Whittaker Chambers who said they had belonged to the same communist underground. Chambers said that Hiss took home State Department documents and had his wife, Priscilla, type copies of them, which he gave to Chambers. From a pumpkin on his farm near Westminster, Maryland, Chambers produced what no part-time farmer had ever produced before—the Pumpkin Papers, including 58 damning microfilmed pages of documents.

But Hiss said he had never met the man. Much of the testimony against Hiss in the House Un-American Activities Committee hearings, and later at his 1949 trial, revolved around whether Chambers had actually been to his house. To support the assertion, both Chambers and his wife, Esther, came up with descriptive detail on the three rented houses in Georgetown where Hiss and his family had lived in the thirties.

According to Chambers's story, he and Hiss saw each other almost every week, starting in early 1935 when Hiss lived in a Federal-style townhouse at 2905 P Street N.W. Chambers swore that he had spent many nights at their next house, 1245 30th Street N.W., a small rowhouse where the Hisses lived from July 1936 to December 1937. In honor of this previous occupant, a later owner painted the house's interior a pumpkin color and named his dog Pumpkin.

Esther Chambers testified that she was at their next house, a more upscale one at 3415 Volta Place, in the winter of 1938, where she had observed "forsythias cascading" at the front gate. Hiss, who has always maintained his innocence, argued in his book, *In the Court of Public Opinion*, that while she was right about the espaliered bush, even forsythia doesn't bloom *that* early.

Years later, Senator Prescott S. Bush, the President's father, lived in the same house. In other words, at least when visiting his parents, Bush slept here.

When an elusive typewriter of Hiss provenance turned up in a friend's back yard, things did not look good for him. The typewriter had the same type face as the copies of State Department documents that Priscilla Hiss had allegedly made. Hiss was found guilty, not of espionage but of perjury—for denying he had ever met Chambers or given him classified papers. Undaunted, in his appeal, Hiss cast himself as a victim of "forgery by typewriter." He served four years in jail.

Under Covers
Russell J. Bowen Collection
Lauinger Library, Georgetown University
37th and Prospect Streets N.W.

In this country, the Russell J. Bowen Collection of Works on Intelligence, Security and Covert Activities is second only to the CIA in its holdings of intelligence books. The agency owns about 25,000. By comparison, the Bowen Collection, donated to Georgetown University by a retired CIA analyst and bibliophile, numbers a respectable 11,000 volumes.

On the top floor of the Lauinger Library, one shares the small research room with silent scholars who appear surprisingly indifferent to whether anyone sees what titles they are reading. Their interest is purely clinical, a step removed, conjecture. Or so one may assume.

The collection dates back to 1699, to a book by a disgruntled English spy named Matthew South. When his employer in the nobility didn't pay him, he wrote this exposé outlining his activities.

The stacks are closed; books are not available for browsing, so it helps to know in advance what one is looking for. In informal looseleaf notebooks, books are listed by author and title but not subject, rated by the collector and described in thumbnail sketches.

On a PC in the librarians' office, one may also do a keyword search of the data base which duplicates the contents of the notebooks.

The Last Supper of Vitaly Yurchenko
Au Pied de Cochon
1335 Wisconsin Avenue N.W.

Vitaly S. Yurchenko and his CIA guard had a late lunch on Saturday, November 2, 1985.

Yurchenko was a KGB colonel who had defected three months before by walking into the American Embassy in Rome and had been spilling the beans ever since. He imparted a good deal of sensitive information and exposed as KGB agents former CIA officer Edward Lee Howard and former NSA employee Ronald Pelton. But things had not worked out as Yurchenko had hoped. For one thing,

Defector Vitaly Yurchenko made his getaway from this Georgetown bistro. His table was in the corner by the window.

*Soviet KGB colonel Vitaly Yurchenko, the once and former defector,
stands in Moscow's Red Square after his redefection.*

his Russian girlfriend had no intention of leaving her husband. More
important, the defector had been mistreated. Not only had he been
kept a virtual prisoner by the agency, but he had asked that his
defection be kept secret, and CIA director William Casey was bruit-
ing it about town. Their offer of a million dollars and a lifetime
income didn't compensate him enough for his outrage.

Now the defector was sitting at a small table across from his
escort in a Georgetown bistro, Au Pied de Cochon. He was waiting
for his moment. When the waiter came, both men ordered the
poached salmon.

Perhaps the defector was not hungry.

He turned to his guard and said, "I'm going for a walk. If I
don't come back, it's not your fault." He got up and left.

Nonplussed, the security guard sat and waited to pay the check.

"They say he went to the bathroom and went out the back door,"
said the owner of the restaurant, Yves Courbois. "But I could not
tell you. Because when we are so busy there are people going through
the back door to exit sometimes. It's so crazy what's going on here."

In fact, Yurchenko just walked out the front door. Now there's a display over it, touting the Original Yurchenko Shooter, invented by an imaginative bartender. Occasionally a tourist orders the drink—equal parts Grand Marnier and Stolichnaya vodka, served chilled and strained into a snifter. Potent, barely palatable. And there's a plaque on the banquette next to the table where Yurchenko sat—it was busy that night, who could remember the exact table? It took a while for the facts to shake down, what with reporters crawling all over the place. And then the plaque ended up with the wrong date on it. Nonetheless, people with Russian accents still phone up and try to reserve the table where the plaque is, commemorating "Yurchenko's Last Supper in the USA." Does it matter that he didn't actually eat it?

Yurchenko the Revisionist
Former Soviet Embassy buildings
2650 Wisconsin Avenue N.W.

After he left his meal at Au Pied de Cochon, Yurchenko dashed up Wisconsin Avenue to the Russian compound, a little more than a mile away. At night mercury vapor lights harshly illuminate the wide, inhospitable lawn dotted with security cameras and ringed with wrought-iron fencing on a stone wall. Yurchenko apparently had no problems getting through the gate.

Two days later he held a press conference. He said that he hadn't actually defected, he had been kidnapped. Nabbed at the Vatican, he had been taken to America, where he was drugged and held prisoner. His assertions helped fuel the argument of some CIA critics that the KGB had sent Yurchenko to dupe the Americans, to glean information and sow disinformation. After all, back in Russia Colonel Yurchenko had been in the training program for KGB generals.

Embassy-watchers noted with mild interest that Yurchenko, rather than heading for the old embassy downtown, hurried to the

The Russians' beaux-arts mansion on 16th Street.

new complex. It is a veritable village in beige brick and white faux marble. The dwelling places are occupied, but the office buildings aren't supposed to be used until the United States gets a corresponding bug-proof new embassy in Moscow. For their new installation, the Soviets managed to grab the second highest spot in Washington—a too-tempting listening post. As the saying goes in real estate—location, location, location.

Meanwhile, it's embassy business as usual, apparently, at the Russian Embassy at 1125 16th Street N.W., a beaux-arts mansion with gold-leaf and marble interior. It's so much more inviting. At least until the Berlin Wall crumbled, it was more likely to attract zealots and would-be spies walking in or tossing documents over the fence.

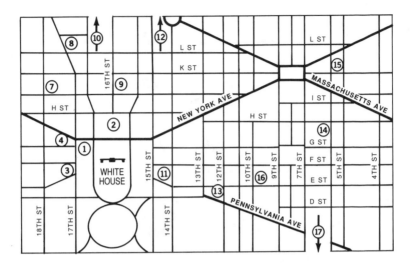

1. The Old Executive Office Building
   17th Street and Pennsylvania Avenue, NW

2. Lafayette Square
   bordered by Pennsylvania Avenue and
   H Street, between 15th and 17th Streets

3. Intelligence Community Staff Headquarters
   1724 F Street, NW

4. The Exchange, Ltd.
   1719 G Street, NW

5. Howard Johnson's Motor Lodge
   2601 Virginia Avenue, NW

6. Watergate
   2600 Virginia Avenue, NW

7. Sidney Kramer Books
   1825 Eye Street, NW

8. Mayflower Hotel
   1127 Connecticut Avenue, NW

9. Site of "Rebel" Rose O. Greenhow's home
   900 block of 16th Street, NW

10. The Iron Gate Inn
    1734 N Street, NW

11. The Willard
    1401 Pennsylvania Avenue, NW

12. Site of the Imperial German Embassy
    1425 Massachusetts Avenue, NW

13. Olsson's Books at Metro Center
    1200 F Street, NW

14. Go-Lo's Restaurant
    604 H Street, NW

15. Steuart Building
    The block between 5th and 6th Streets
    and K Street and New York Avenue

16. Federal Bureau of Investigation Headquarters
    9th and E Streets, NW

17. FBI II
    Washington Metropolitan Field Office
    1900 Half Street, SW

18. Danker's Restaurant
    6th and D Streets, SW

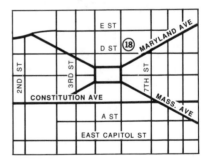

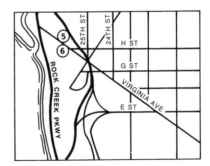

Codebreaker
The Old Executive Office Building
17th Street and Pennsylvania Avenue N.W.

It was a trademark gambit of Herbert O. Yardley to fall asleep musing on a code that needed solving and to wake up in the middle of the night with the eureka-solution. His success in codes was attributed to his early training by professional poker players in the saloons of Worthington, Indiana, where he grew up.

National Archives

View of the State, War and Navy Building's south, or State Department, side in 1913, when cryptologist Herbert O. Yardley first went to work in the Code Room on the first floor. It is now the Old Executive Office Building.

27

Yardley, the most colorful of American cryptologists, got his start in the code room of the State, War and Navy Building, now known as the Old Executive Office Building. In 1913, Yardley was a young telegraph operator working out of a State Department office on the first floor. "This spacious room with its high ceiling over-looked the southern White House grounds," he recalled in his autobiography, *The American Black Chamber*. "By lifting my eyes from my work I could see a tennis game in progress where a few years earlier President Roosevelt and his tennis Cabinet had played each day."

This room was most likely one of the offices that the National Service Bureau currently occupies, and a recent visit suggests that, if Yardley did get a look at the tennis courts from the recessed windows, he was not only a cryptologist, but a contortionist. Poetic license, perhaps.

While working there, coding and decoding military and diplomatic cipher telegrams, Yardley observed that the State Department's codes were essentially the same as those used in the 16th century. Another World War I code clerk, humorist James Thurber, characterized these codes as "a system of deception as easy to see through as the passing attack of a grammar school football team."

In his spare time, Yardley would solve codes to impress his superiors by showing how simple it was. Armed with decoded telegrams, he persuaded the War Department, shortly after the Americans entered World War I, to start a cryptologic service. Located briefly in the War College Building at what is now known as Fort McNair, this service became MI-8, the cryptographic section of the Military Intelligence Division. Yardley headed the section. But encoding and decoding our own telegrams was a bit tame for him. What Yardley really wanted, and what he got, was a black chamber. He opened it in 1919 in a Manhattan brownstone.

Back as far as the 17th century, the French had had its *Cabinet Noir* for reading the ciphered messages of foreign diplomats. In the 1920s, some considered the black chamber a legacy of the Middle Ages—certainly out of place in peacetime. In 1929, the new Secretary of State, Henry L. Stimson, thought so when he closed down Yardley's black chamber and later explained, "Gentlemen do not read each other's mail." By then, according to the cryptologist's putative successor, William F. Friedman, Yardley was devoting most of his time

This photo of Captain Herbert O. Yardley was taken in 1918 when he was chief of MI-8 of the Military Intelligence Division.

to "private enterprises." In short, he was "having a field day at government expense."

Perhaps it was another bit of poetic license that led Yardley to reveal in his autobiography two years later that his black chamber team had broken the diplomatic codes and ciphers of 20 countries. (Put on their guard, the countries' overwhelming response was to revamp their cryptographic systems.) The powers that be decided he went too far when he masterminded the ghostwritten book, *Japanese Diplomatic Secrets: 1921–22*, based on intercepted Japanese messages that had been decoded in the black chamber. A ponderous 970-pager, the Justice Department seized it before the publisher had time to read it. Now it rests in manila envelopes in the National Archives.

Among other careers, Yardley took a flier in real estate development, and he set up a code department for General Chiang Kai-Shek. He never gave up poker. He died in Silver Spring, Maryland, in 1958.

He is not missed by NSA types, who swear he couldn't get a clearance today. After all, he did the unforgiveable—told what he knew, for profit, and even had *The American Black Chamber* serialized in the *Saturday Evening Post*.

Note: For Saturday tours of the Old Executive Office Building that focus on recent restoration work, call (202)395-5895.

Watching Abe Lincoln
Lafayette Square
Pennsylvania Avenue and H Streets N.W., between 15th and 17th Streets

No doubt spies have quietly come and gone from the famous park across from the White House. We'll never know who most of them were, but in days of looser security, the object of their surveillance was obvious. In 1864, one such agent was the Rebel scout Thomas Nelson Conrad. A member of a plot to kidnap Lincoln and take him to Richmond, thus to throw the Union into turmoil, he spent his days waiting in the park.

Today's would-be spies could take a page from his autobiography, albeit self-indulgent, on the how-tos of blending into the woodwork:

> In a city crowded with hostile soldiers, guards at the entrances and pickets at outposts, detectives at every point and house servants suspicious, it seems amazing that a rebel scout could enter and remain for days without detection and capture! And yet the author . . . moved around generally as any citizen would. He sought to conform to the dress and movement of the average man. He avoided hotel lobbies, restaurants and barrooms.

For his forays into Washington, Conrad dressed in a chaplain's suit.

Lincoln had made the Soldiers' Home on the northern outskirts of the city his summer retreat. The President would leave the Executive Mansion in the cool of the evening in his private carriage and be driven directly to the Soldiers' Home, where he usually spent the night. As Conrad watched Lincoln's movements to and from the White House, the evening departure seemed the logical time to strike.

However, word must have gotten out, for security was abruptly increased. "Imagine my astounding surprise and total collapse," Conrad wrote, "when we beheld the carriage of Mr. Lincoln moving out of the grounds of the White House preceded and followed by a squad of cavalry."

In the summer of 1866, Conrad settled in Upperville, Virginia, and married Miss Minnie Ball. He noted with amusement in his memoirs that her name sounded the same as the Minié ball that was shot from Civil War rifles, but he didn't say whether she lived up to it.

Intelligence Central
Intelligence Community Staff Headquarters
1724 F Street N.W.

The "intelligence community" sounds like a nebulous form, but it's an integrated body of 12 parts. Two blocks from the White House, one of the more elegant townhomes in the business district is the headquarters of the Intelligence Community staff. The staff helps the director of Central Intelligence (a.k.a. the director of the CIA) coordinate the activities of the intelligence community. It keeps NSA from tripping over the CIA and so forth, but mainly, it exists because of increased efforts to coordinate intelligence that date at least as far back as the Pearl Harbor post mortems. The organizations that make up the community are the CIA, FBI, NSA, the National Reconnaissance Office (NRO), the Defense Intelligence Agency (DIA), and intelligence components of the Departments of Energy, Treasury and State and the Army, Navy, Air Force and Marines.

It's the job of the CIA to centralize the intelligence from all of them—to analyze the information from sources such as intercepts, human spies and satellites and come up with unified judgments about what it all means.

When all this coordinating gives them an appetite, they may go across the street to Maison Blanche, 1725 F Street N.W., which offers a very nice early-bird *prix fixe* dinner on weeknights for $24.95. For lunch, there are always roast beef sandwiches, fish and chips, and omelettes at The Exchange, 1719 G Street N.W.

Swinging Spies
The Exchange, Ltd.
1719 G Street N.W.

They say there is no espionage without sex. KGB spy Karl Koecher and his wife, Hana, embodied the adage. He was a mole in the CIA; she was a courier for Czech Intelligence.

In the mid-1970s, the Koechers belonged to a swinging couples group, Capitol Couples, which met informally at The Exchange on Saturday nights. With its convenient downtown location, The Exchange proved an easy way of meeting like-minded folks, because who wants to waste time with formalities when they're on a tight congressional schedule? The Capitol Couples would repair from the restaurant to a hotel or private home for group sex. In those pre-AIDS days, the Koechers used such outlets as one more source of information. At a private club called Virginia's In Place, for example, at least ten of the partygoers worked for the CIA.

Karl Koecher was a Czech Intelligence Service officer who became a naturalized U.S. citizen in 1971. In 1973, he became a CIA translator with a top-secret clearance. On trips to Europe, Hana Koecher, who was a diamond merchant, would pick up the payments for his stolen documents.

He was the typical "illegal," an agent of a hostile intelligence service who infiltrates another country's intelligence service without ever appearing to have ties with his original employer. When developing his legend or cover story, he neglected to mention that he had joined the Communist Party in 1960 and that before he arrived in this country in 1965, he had trained with Czech Intelligence.

Among Koecher's haunts here were his flat at 3100 Manchester Street in Falls Church, Virginia, and the towpath along the C&O Canal. A short man who looked like a fox with his red beard, he was an avid jogger along the wooded towpath. He was not to be seen in these parts after 1986, however. After being confronted by the FBI, the Koechers were traded along with others for Soviet dissident Natan Sharansky and returned to Czechoslovakia.

Strangely, the Koechers were incensed at having to give up their U.S. citizenship.

A Black-Bag Job
Howard Johnson's Motor Lodge
2601 Virginia Avenue N.W.

When five burglars were arrested for breaking into the Democratic National Committee (DNC) headquarters on June 17, 1972, a major chapter in domestic spying was written. The ultimate responsibility for this assignment was the hot potato that bounced from hand to hand throughout the Watergate hearings and eventually led to Richard Nixon's resignation.

The DNC was renting the sixth floor of the Watergate building at 2600 Virginia Avenue N.W. Across the street at Howard Johnson's, James McCord had taken a room. A retired CIA employee, McCord was working as security officer for the Republican National Committee and the Committee to Re-Elect the President (CRP). He and a few fellow burglars broke into the DNC and installed taps on the phones.

For three weeks, first in Room 419, then in Room 723—from which there was a much better view—another CRP employee, Alfred C. Baldwin III, monitored the Democrats' phone calls. Numbering about 200, some of the conversations dealt with political strategy, and some were personal, intimate in fact. According to an interview that Baldwin gave the *Los Angeles Times*, DNC secretaries sometimes used one of the tapped phones in the mistaken belief that it was a more private extension.

As the Democrats often worked into the night, Baldwin spent many hours staring at a horizontal line on the video display terminal on his monitoring unit. When the line broke up, that meant someone was using the phone. Baldwin would put on the earphones. He kept logs of the conversations he monitored and typed them up for McCord.

USW 967-72

SUPERIOR COURT OF THE DISTRICT OF COLUMBIA

AFFIDAVIT IN SUPPORT OF AN APPLICATION FOR A SEARCH WARRANT

For the Premises known as Room 214 and room 314 , Watergate Hotel, 2650 Va., Ave., N.W., Washington, D.C. and a Vehicle known as a 1972 Chrysler, Black in color bearing Va. Tags U 4690, now located in the basement of the Watergate Complex.

On June 17,1972, while asigned to Cr. 727 monitored a radio run to assist the the security guard at 2600 Va. Ave.,N.W. . Arrived at approximately 0210 hours interviewed security guard Frank Mills, at this time responded to the door that leads to the basement garage the door had tape over the lock at this time the guard stated that the 8th floor had been entered in the past month.

Sgt. Leaper, Officer Barrett and Officer Carl Schoffler started to check the buildi The eighth floor had tape on the lock also after searching entire eighth floor,responde to the next sixth floor which also had been set up with tape on the lock after a searc of the first office Officer Barrett, Sgt.Leaper and Officer Carl Schoffler went into an ajoining office. Officer Barrett confronted several subjects hiding behind a screen at this time the above mentioned Officer asked the subjects to come out. One of the subjects said " You got us". The subjectshad their hands in the air. They were wearing surgical gloves the subjects were searched and all had cannisters of Mace also in their possession were lock picks and other burglary tools, also pocket flash lights when the subjects were requested to raise their hands recovered on a desk by the s subjects was a brief case containing two cameras and a large amount of fast film and camera ligh also found in the brief case was a devise which appeared to be the body of a bomb.

Upon searching the above mentioned subjects keys to rooms 314 and 214 of the Water te Hotel, 2650 Va. Ave.,N.W. were found.

In addition, upon searching the above mentioned subjects a key to an Avis Rent-A-car, a Chrysler sedan, Va. Tags U4690 was found. Investigation revealed the above car was parked in basement of Watergate complex.

is ██

The above mentioned subjects refused to give any information besides names ,at leastone of which proved to be false based on a FBI fingerprint check.

Upon checking with the management of the Watergate Hotel it was determined that th of the persons using the same names as those given to the Police at the time of arrest checked into the above rooms on June 16,1972.

██ ██ ███████████

Upon checking with Avis Rent-A - Car it was determined that the Chrysler Sedan Va. Tags U 4690 , was rented on June 16,1972, by one Bernard L. Barker, which name one of the above subjects later gave at Second District Headquarters. The sixth floor office is occupied by the Demo.Nat'l.Comm.,which did nost give anyone per-nission Based on the foregoing information the affiant has reason to believe that the abov to premises and car contain the following evidence and instrumentalies of the crime of ter Burglary Two: Burglary tools, Electronic Surveilance devices other toools complimentar to those found on the scene, maps and other plans friction tape,fringerprints, documen and other evidence of identification, incendary and bomb manufacturing devices and implements and other instrumentalies and evidence of crime.

Carl M Shoffle

CARL M SHOFFLER

SUBSCRIBED AND SWORN TO BEFORE ME THIS ___ DAY OF _____ 1972

_____

JUDGE, SUPERIOR COURT OF THE DISTRICT OF COLUMBIA.   LC- 1

Just after the Watergate break-in, D.C. officer Carl Shoffler found the keys to two Watergate Hotel rooms in the pockets of the DNC burglars. He filed this affidavit in support of his application for a warrant to search the rooms.

From a room in Howard Johnson's, eavesdroppers from the Committee to Re-Elect the President listened in to the phone calls of the Democratic National Committee headquarters at the Watergate building across the street.

Apparently the taps didn't net enough information. On the night of June 16, McCord came to Baldwin's room carrying a bag full of bugging devices and the tools to install them. He proudly brandished a listening device—some door chimes—and took it with him when he left. From his balcony at HoJo's, Baldwin watched McCord cross the street to the Watergate building.

Baldwin's job that night was surveillance. He was to keep an eye out for anything unusual and to communicate same by walkie-talkie to the burglars across the street. This is what he did when he saw two strange men walk out onto the balcony of the DNC carrying guns. But it was too late to warn the burglars. By then, the police, alerted by a security guard, were all over the place.

The Watergate burglars were arrested wearing rubber surgical gloves, carrying $2,300 in sequentially numbered hundred-dollar bills and toting their bugging devices. Moments after their arrest, former CIA man E. Howard Hunt rushed into Room 723 at HoJo's, found out what had happened from Baldwin and called a lawyer. Hunt was one of the White House secret agents known as "the plumbers," who were to investigate news leaks, and whose dirty-tricks campaign was aimed at ensuring Nixon's re-election. Hunt was also known for sporting a red wig, a disguise which the CIA had supplied.

Bookworm Cowboy
Sidney Kramer Books
1825 Eye Street N.W.

As director of the CIA from 1981 to 1987, William J. Casey stood at the helm during the Iran-Contra scandal and involved the agency in it. In failing to adequately inform Congress of the CIA's activities, he typified the "cowboy" approach. In intelligence jargon, cowboys have a certain reckless disregard for anything beyond their own agenda—fighting the Soviets, in his case.

If Casey had a spare moment he was likely to mosey over to his favorite bookstore, Sidney Kramer Books, when it was on H Street. The store has since moved to a newer building, but Casey's penchant for reading was so phenomenal it's still worth mentioning. He spent more money on books in a year than most people's annual salary—between $40,000 and $60,000. CIA security guards had to carry the books to his car.

Herb Meyer, a former special assistant to Casey, said the late DCI once dropped $68 at a newsstand in New York City. "He would say, 'Don't you read this?'" Casey would have in his hand some obscure journal like the *Luxembourg Quarterly*.

Casey always seemed to be the first to read a new book—often while it was still in galley proofs. His tastes ran to politics and economics. And, Meyer noted, "There were dozens of newsletters and magazines that Casey was the only known subscriber to."

Hoover Ate Here
Harvey's Restaurant
(site at 1001 18th Street N.W.)
The Mayflower Hotel
1127 Connecticut Avenue N.W.

No wonder J. Edgar Hoover had high blood pressure. His work day began at 8:30 A.M., after a breakfast of bacon, eggs, fruit juice, toast and coffee.

"He seldom leaves his office before 7," a 1953 *Newsweek* article noted. "Then he goes to Harvey's Restaurant on Connecticut Avenue, where a table is always reserved for him, a table for four, but with only two chairs. His dinner companion invariably is Clyde Tolson, number-two man in the FBI, who, according to the report, is also his armed bodyguard.

"At Harvey's, Hoover generally orders steak or roast beef, which he often tops off with a Caesar salad. . ."

J. Edgar Hoover meets his match in a prize bulldog.

The director of the FBI was worried about the "Red menace" but not about his cholesterol. During his half-century of iron-fist rule, some of the bigger spies the bureau caught were the Rosenbergs and the Nazi saboteurs who landed on Long Island from U-boats during World War II.

Harvey's used to be in a three-story building where the Connecticut Connection is now. According to Alex Stuart, a former Harvey's owner, Hoover's table was just inside the door, underneath the stairway to the second floor. It was probably the most secure spot in the building. "You couldn't see it right away when you came in," said Stuart.

But Hoover had stopped going there when Stuart bought it. Harvey's Restaurant then moved to 18th Street. "We just missed him" in the new location, Stuart said. Too bad. Hoover would have loved the subterranean labyrinth of candlelit booths, nooks, crannies, corners and exits.

There was some controversy about this spycatcher's philosophy that every once in a while—dinnertime, anyway—rank has its privileges. In his book *The Director*, Ovid Demaris said that Hoover "did enjoy a free ride at Harvey's for the 20-odd years that Julius Lulley owned it." His last waiter there was William Holley, from 1951 to 1965. The waiter told Demaris that Hoover "never saw a check." Then another owner, Jesse Brinkman, bought Harvey's, "and they didn't go for all this freeloading stuff," Demaris wrote. "They sent him a bill in the mail. His visits tapered off, and finally he just stopped coming completely."

Another favorite eatery for Hoover was at The Mayflower Hotel. According to Frank Glaine, the hotel's director of special markets, "There used to be an old men's bar there where Hoover and Tolson used to eat. He had a special table in the Rib Room," which has since been replaced by the Nicholas restaurant. When Hoover died, they didn't use his table for a whole week. "We draped it with black crepe," Glaine said.

Rebel Rose
Site of Rose O. Greenhow's home
900 block of 16th Street N.W.

The Civil War in Washington was a high-water mark for female spies. While the men went off to war, some of the women back home mixed up a conspiratorial brew. The grandmother of spies was "Rebel Rose"—the widow Rose O'Neal Greenhow, who had grown up in Montgomery County and made her debut on Capitol Hill. During the war she resided in a small house at 398 16th Street N.W. House numbers in the District have changed around since then, and that would place her house next to the Sheraton-Carlton Hotel (923 16th Street N.W.), where a patio with tea tables is located now. She was just up the street from St. John's Episcopal Church, Lafayette Park and the White House. She had known nine presidents in all. Entertaining senators and cabinet members, she was an early Perle Mesta, the prototypical doyenne of Washington society—but with a deadly purpose.

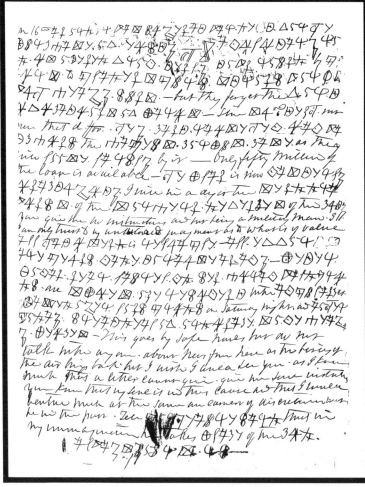

This "correspondence of a treasonable nature" was found in Rose O'Neal Greenhow's possession.

Rose Greenhow would sit with her visitor on the striped damask chairs in one of her parlors (there were two of them, divided by red gauze), or she would take him to the back room and play for him on her rosewood pianoforte, long lovely fingers stroking the pearl keys. There were dinners—terrapin, oysters and wild turkey with champagne, followed by sherry cobbler. While they dined, she picked his brain—right in line with that Washington adage, "There's no such thing as a free lunch."

She considered her greatest achievement to be her involvement in the first battle of Manassas/Bull Run, which took place about 25

A FEMALE SPY.

A woodcut from THE SPY OF THE REBELLION, written by Allan Pinkerton, head of McClellan's secret service bureau. Pinkerton nabbed Confederate agent Rose O'Neal Greenhow.

Allan Pinkerton (seated, holding a cigar), head of General George B. McClellan's secret service, confers with his officers in this Mathew Brady photo.

miles from the city. Greenhow was part of a spy network set up by Thomas Jordan, who taught her to communicate in cipher and who went on to be General Pierre G.T. Beauregard's adjutant general. The spy ring included a banker, a dentist and young women who acted as messengers.

The story goes that one such messenger, Betty Duvall, concealed Rose's fateful cipher message to Beauregard in her chignon and, when she got to camp, let her hair down. The message was that the Federals had decided to move into Virginia. Beauregard had time to reposition some of his troops before McDowell's advance on Manassas.

As Greenhow later recalled joyously in her memoirs, "Crimination and recrimination now became the order of the day," as the "craven Yankees" retreated from Manassas after a rout. Rose reveled. Jordan sent her this note: "Our President and our General direct me to thank you. We rely upon you for further information. The Confederacy owes you a debt."

Though encouraged and more defiant than ever, she was not able to repeat the feat. Little more than a month later, she encountered Allan Pinkerton, a.k.a. Major E. J. Allen, head of General George B. McClellan's secret service bureau, which was just around the corner at 17th and Eye Streets. Eavesdropping reached new heights when Pinkerton took off his shoes and stood on the shoulders of two of his men to peer through her parlor window and listen to one of her "sensitive" conversations.

Pinkerton arrested her in front of her house as she was "returning from a promenade," she said. She had the foresight to swallow a "very important note." Other suspicious notes and maps found in her home are in the National Archives.

When he placed her under house arrest, her 16th Street home became known in the press as "Fort Greenhow." A few months later, she and her eight-year-old daughter, also named Rose, were moved to the more secure Old Capitol Prison, where they experienced "more outrages than Marie Antoinette."

Undaunted, she continued to send messages—probably riddled with disinformation in case Pinkerton read them. She recalled in her memoirs "certain Federal officers, whom I induced without scruple. . .to furnish me with information, even in my captivity, which information I at once communicated with pride and pleasure to General Beauregard. . . ."

Finally, she was sent South, the worst that could happen to a female spy in the Union capital in a time when, in general, spies were tolerated and women patronized. She went to England to publish her memoirs and to act as informal ambassador for the Confederacy. On her return in 1864, her ship ran aground. Impetuous as ever, she insisted on being taken ashore in a small boat. It capsized and she drowned—weighted down by a bag of gold coins, the money she'd made on her book.

The Defector and the Call Girl
The Iron Gate Inn
1734 N Street N.W., Rear

It was Columbus Day 1978 when Soviet defector Arkady Shevchenko was ambushed at lunch at the Iron Gate Inn, one of Washington's first Middle Eastern restaurants, a remodeled stable off N Street. In the courtyard, deserted because of the holiday, Shevchenko sat down at a table and ordered a double vodka. He was waiting for his girlfriend. She was a call girl named Judy Chavez, whom he had met through an escort service. He had bought her a car, taken her to the Virgin Islands, and was paying her $5,000 a month.

The former advisor to Soviet Foreign Minister Andrei Gromyko and, more recently, United Nations Under Secretary General, Shevchenko was not used to being kept waiting. When he came in from the cold six months before, he was the highest ranking diplomat ever to defect from the Soviet Union. The CIA gave him the usual defector treatment—a bodyguard, a driver, an undisclosed sum of money.

Sitting at his table under the trees, perhaps Shevchenko thought to order the stuffed grape leaves. Anyway, his double vodka came.

But Chavez didn't show. She sent an NBC camera crew in her place. After a few hasty words with NBC News, Shevchenko took off.

"I had been mistaken and naive in trusting Chavez's sincerity

45

and good intentions," Shevchenko said in his book, *Breaking with Moscow*. Apparently, she knew a good story when she saw one, and her own version of events came out in paperback. Contrary to her assertion that he supported her with his government stipend, Shevchenko insisted he had paid her with his own money.

Asked for comment, a CIA spokesman sounded a note of measured indifference: "What he does with his money is his business."

Cloak and Swagger
The Willard
1401 Pennsylvania Avenue N.W.

In the 19th century, the lobby of the old Willard Hotel was the traditional gathering place for Washington's movers and shakers—so much so that Ulysses S. Grant coined the word lobbyist there. Although the Willard has been elegantly transformed from the squat building it was then, the lobby has always been in the same location. It was the scene of the recruitment of Lafayette C. Baker, who would become the infamous counterespionage officer of the Civil War era.

In early 1861, he ran into two Union friends with whom he "conversed freely upon the condition of the country, and the necessity of more reliable information respecting the strength and movements of the enemy." And, egotist that he was, he saw the point they were trying to make: He was indeed, as he wrote, "the man of all others to go into this secret service."

His friends then escorted him to the rooms of General-in-Chief Winfield Scott. Thus began a series of meetings at the Willard. According to Baker's memoirs, the Union general grumbled about not being able to learn about Rebel forces at Manassas. He recruited Baker to find his way south on an intelligence-gathering mission.

As it turned out, Baker's future lay in counterintelligence. After his foray south, he became chief of a small force of detectives that was the closest thing to a Union secret service. As special provost

Counterintelligence officer Lafayette C. Baker, whose own opinion of himself surpassed his reputation as "the terror of all rogues," in a photo from his 1867 autobiography.

marshal and special agent for the War Department, he attempted to ferret out Secessionist sympathizers, investigating cases of disloyalty, treason and vandalism. In the high point of his career, he headed the search for John Wilkes Booth and investigated the Lincoln assassination.

"He was the terror of all rogues," observed the chaplain of "Baker's Cavalry," his regiment. As most arrested Secessionists were released upon taking the loyalty oath, and those refusing were merely forwarded to Dixie, Baker's bark was worse than his bite.

His reputation for over-zealous pursuit of his mandate can be attributed to his spying on President Andrew Johnson, who tossed him out of the White House. He testified against Johnson in his impeachment hearings. Baker's reputation for ruthlessness naturally followed from his sanctimonious self-inflation. The introduction to his memoirs, *The History of the United States Secret Service*, contains this modest description of himself:

> In General Baker's personal appearance there is nothing, to a casual observer, remarkable. And yet, physically, he is an extraordinary man. . . .He is probably the best "shot" in the country, and. . .has never been addicted to the shameless profanity so common in the army and among men of adventurous character.

The Zimmermann Telegram
Site of the Imperial German Embassy
1425 Massachusetts Avenue N.W.

During World War I and through the early 1940s, the German embassy was located on the northeast corner of 15th Street and Massachusetts Avenue N.W., now a parking lot. Long-time tenants of the Heatherington Apartments next door, women who have lived there since the embassy was razed, swear that a tunnel led from it and that the parking lot was laid over a warren of underground rooms. Such matters await confirmation by archaeological excavation.

In the midst of the capital of a country trying to remain neutral in the Great War, the embassy was the setting for intrigue. Early in the war, Captain Franz von Papen served as the military attaché. While his mornings started with a ride on horseback in Rock Creek Park, the rest of his day was not so bucolic. Running a spy system out of the United States, Papen tried to delay troop transport from Canada to Europe. To that end, he plotted to blow up key points in the Canadian-Pacific Railway line. For the bridge over the Welland

Canal, he paid his agent $500. He should've paid more; the attempt misfired. He also supplied false passports and sent home lists of American arms shipments.

In the event that America entered the war, Papen was to open his safe in the embassy, take out a long, thick envelope, break the seals and find instructions for his course of action. But he was saved the trouble. In December 1915, because of his espionage activities, Papen got himself declared *persona non grata*, along with the naval attaché, Karl Boy-Ed. Papen would go on to serve as chancellor of Germany and ambassador to Turkey, among other posts, and to become one of the few Nazi officials to be acquitted at the Nuremberg trials.

The ambassador, Count Johann von Bernstorff, stayed on, of course, when his two attachés were recalled. On January 16, 1917, he played a role in the historic affair of the Zimmermann Telegram. On that day, German foreign minister Arthur Zimmermann sent him an encoded message to be forwarded to the German minister in Mexico. The count decoded it and then re-encoded the message in a simpler code he knew the minister to have. It is a crime in cryptology to send the same message in two different codes, and this maxim would be perfectly illustrated for the count.

The Zimmermann Telegram proposed an alliance with Mexico in the event the Americans entered the war. In exchange, Germany would help Mexico regain its lands in Texas, New Mexico and Arizona. An alliance with Japan was also proposed.

Unbeknownst to the Germans, the British had intercepted and decoded the telegram along the way. There were gaps in their first decryption, but the count's new coding helpfully cleared these up. Conveniently, the British knew someone in the Mexican telegraph office. Five weeks later, the decryption complete, the British presented the American ambassador to the Court of St. James with a copy of the telegram. Then, on March 1, newspapers published the telegram's contents. Americans were galvanized, and entry into World War I became a certainty. By then, Count von Bernstorff was already on his way home.

Eyes Only
Olsson's Books at Metro Center
1200 F Street N.W.

This outlet of the Olsson's chain is where the spooks and would-be spooks stock up. Look for them during off-hours here, scoping out the large section on intelligence. It takes up the same amount of space as mysteries, biographies or sci-fi. Among the usual popular fiction and non-fiction techno-crypto-intelligence books, you may also find such tradecraft delectations as *How to Create a New Identity* (author anonymous, of course), the tersely titled *Bribes, The Big Book of Secret Hiding Places* and *How to Disappear Completely and Never Be Found* (don't try this before leaving the store).

If you don't see what you want on the shelves, you may want to consult the insiders' catalog and newsletter, *Surveillant*, published by the National Intelligence Book Center, 1700 K Street N.W. 20006. These books may be ordered through Olsson's special ears-only number, (202) 337-8084. Calls may be traced.

"The Nest That Hatched the Egg"
Go-Lo's Restaurant
604 H Street N.W.

Go-Lo's Restaurant dishes up a notable chowfoon—wide rice noodles tossed with meat or seafood and vegetables. It is also known for having been Mary Surratt's boarding house, where the Lincoln conspirators met and sometimes stayed over. (See page 108.) A federal-style house, Go-Lo's in Chinatown has the original tin roof but a modern interior painted rose

The Lincoln conspirators met at Mary Surratt's boarding house on
H Street, N.W. It is now a Chinese restaurant.

and gray-green. Lunch is served on those ubiquitous Chinese zodiac placemats. Note that Mary Surratt was born in 1823, the Year of the Sheep, and John Wilkes Booth in 1838, the Year of the Dog. Tells you something about their relationship.

Acting as an agent for the Confederacy, Booth initially was part of a plan to kidnap President Lincoln and hold him hostage for a massive release of Confederate prisoners. But when the Civil War was ending and he saw his side losing, he changed his plan to assassination. "I struck boldly," he wrote in his journal.

Federal prosecutors were unable to make their case that Booth was acting as an agent of the Confederacy when he killed Lincoln on April 14, 1865. The question, posed again in the 1988 book *Come Retribution: The Confederate Secret Service and the Assassination of Lincoln*, remains unanswerable, though, as the authors point out, Booth was "still working the clandestine apparatus" on his escape route.

Part of that apparatus-in-place was Surratt's Tavern, a safehouse in Southern Maryland that the widow Mary Surratt owned.

Around midnight on April 17, while a crowd gathered outside the H Street boarding house, Surratt was arrested and taken to the Old Capitol Prison. Within the month, she went to the Washington Arsenal Penitentiary (now Fort McNair—see page 66), where she would be tried and hanged with three other co-conspirators on July 7, 1865.

President Andrew Johnson said, "She kept the nest that hatched the egg." But the ultimate question of her guilt—just how much she knew—has never been resolved.

Have You Driven a U-2 Lately?
Steuart Building
The block between Fifth and Sixth Streets, and K Street and New York Avenue N.W.

You say you want a deal? There's a beauty sitting out in this lot. True, it's got a lot of mileage on it,

Pamela Kessler

On the top floors of the Steuart Motor Company, the CIA's Photographic Interpretation Center scrutinized U-2 aerial reconnaissance photos.

the used Steuart Ford building. But this isn't just any defunct car dealership. That's just the part that's low to the ground. This baby has hidden features. Under the roof, the top four floors are the former location of the CIA's Photographic Interpretation Center.

Back in the late fifties and sixties when the salesmen were sweating it out down in the showroom, a few floors above them interpreters were poring over aerial reconnaissance pictures spread out on huge boards. The downstairs neighbors were kept in the dark. When couriers guarded by men with machine guns rushed past to deliver their U-2 photos, the people at Ford just assumed the government was printing money up there.

Arthur Lundahl, who ran the center, had purposely chosen the site for the top-secret operation in a rundown neighborhood. It was the perfect cover. Winos would just think they'd had too much to drink when shiny limousines pulled up and dropped off people like Richard Nixon and John Foster Dulles. For briefings on the latest photos, the dignitaries had to step over garbage to enter the building.

In 1962, the analysts made what was possibly the biggest technical intelligence coup in the history of the CIA: They found missiles at Cuban bases. No doubt afterwards some of them went out to celebrate over white pizza in the smoke-filled A-V Ristorante. The legendary A-V is still there, of course, but no telling how long the old Steuart Ford building will be, with its boarded-up bays and broken windows. Sure you're not interested in a monument to the Cuban Missile Crisis?

A Nickel's Worth of Microfilm
Federal Bureau of Investigation Headquarters
Ninth and E Streets N.W.

No amount of piped-in music, of Andy Williams singing "Moon River," can compensate for the humorless world of monitors and mirrors the visitor sees on the FBI building tour. The low ceilings are weighty with justice—or suspicion. At the photos of the ten-most-wanted fugitives, our perky guide Katrina notes that past tourists trekking through have identified at least two such fugitives. Everyone looks a little closer at the photographs.

"There's always a chance," she teases.

Sterile exhibits outline the FBI's six main concerns: drugs, organized crime, white collar crime, violent crime, terrorism and counterintelligence. The exhibit hall is clearly remote from the reality of investigations. Tourists don't penetrate the sensitive areas of the building. The tour offers only a glimpse into the forensics laboratories such as the document section, where bank robbers' demand notes are examined, and the material analysis unit, which looks like a hardware store with its display of paint chips and duct tape.

The FBI is responsible for investigating espionage by Americans: A third of its agents are engaged in counterintelligence orchestrated from within these forbidding walls. On the tour, this is the part where the cloak-and-dagger fan gives full attention. But it's a cursory view; you don't learn much about how the FBI caught whom they caught. You do get to watch a blurry FBI surveillance tape of two Soviet spies during what was called "Operation Lemonade." And you see concealment devices for cleverly storing and passing microfilm: a pencil, a nail, a pen, a cufflink, a doll in peasant dress, a nickel. Inside just such a hollow nickel, a newsboy found microfilmed instructions belonging to KGB master spy Rudolph Abel.

Beyond the tour, it is possible to get a little closer to the gritty. By appointment, the public may examine certain FBI files in the Freedom of Information (FOI) Library. Released in response to FOI requests, many of the files are from J. Edgar Hoover's confidential files. For whatever reason, these he kept separate from the usual FBI indexes. Some say he was packing away these snippets of gossip and innuendo for "insurance"; his supporters have claimed he set them aside to protect the subjects.

Among the FOI pre-processed files, you'll find such names as Bonnie Parker, John Dillinger, Jimi Hendrix, Janis Joplin, Marilyn Monroe, Martin Luther King, Al Capone, Nelson Rockefeller, Albert Einstein, John Hinckley, Clark Gable and, of course, Elvis. The Hoover files alone amount to 11,387 pages.

FBI II
Washington Metropolitan Field Office
1900 Half Street S.W.

While F.B.I. headquarters masterminds the outfit, the agents have to hang their fedoras somewhere—locally, that's the Washington Metropolitan Field Office, a huge cement monolith beyond the derelict trolley tracks. Down and dirty on Buzzard Point, the area is your typical movie chase scene of rutted roads, grubby underpasses, empty warehouses and deserted marinas. It may be down at the heels, but it's home to 20 counterintelligence squads each assigned to a different area or specialty, such as China, Cuba, Russia, the KGB and the GRU (Russian military intelligence). Don't expect any building tours here.

Schmoozing
Danker's Restaurant
Sixth and D Streets S.W.

Urban renewal has uprooted Danker's Restaurant from its longtime location on E Street where it was a favorite hangout for FBI types and Justice Department lawyers. But the oldtimers still find their way to the new place. One of the regulars who won't be coming back, however, is Vitaly Yurchenko. Owner Richard Danker remembers when Yurchenko used to come in, back when he worked for the Soviet embassy. Yurchenko was the KGB colonel who defected to this country in 1985, the year of the spy, only to redefect mysteriously three months later. (See pages 20–22.) He had apparently gotten his taste for America when, from 1975 to 1980, he was the security officer at the Soviet embassy. He used to go to Danker's to meet Ed Joyce, who was the FBI's liaison with him.

"They would stand at the end of the bar and laugh and tell stories, mostly a social time, to let loose from work," Danker says.

One night, Joyce introduced Yurchenko to John L. Martin, a former FBI agent who is chief of the internal security section at Justice. As the government's top spy catcher, Martin has presided over the prosecution of more than 50 spies since 1975. Only one has gotten away.

"John's the guy who puts your spies in jail," Joyce said to Yurchenko.

"Always he is trying to fan the flames of the Cold War and spy mania," Yurchenko said, laughing. "He knows we have no spies."

Back then, Danker didn't know who Yurchenko was. "I knew he was Russian, by the name. I didn't realize he was with the Soviet Embassy. Obviously, there was an accent. You could tell he was Eastern bloc. He wasn't real loud. He didn't go out of his way to meet other people."

Scotch on the rocks was his drink, Danker says. One time Yurchenko ordered a Bloody Mary and fished the ice cubes out, saying that putting ice in drinks was what caused Americans to have so many colds. In all, he wasn't much of a drinker. Joyce says Yurchenko was the type to nurse a drink, seemed always on his guard, and therefore not to be fully trusted.

Besides Yurchenko, another regular they're not likely to see again at Danker's is Nicholas Shadrin. A Soviet naval officer who defected, he was working for the Defense Intelligence Agency when he was sent as a double agent to Vienna for a meeting with the KGB. That was in 1975, and he hasn't been heard from since. Yurchenko himself may have cleared up the mystery. When he defected in 1985, he told the CIA that Shadrin had been chloroformed by the Soviets and that they accidentally gave him too much, killing him.

Shadrin used to eat at Dankers two or three times a week. "He'd have a luncheon steak. Shadrin was a regular with Kay," Danker says, referring to one of several tenured waitresses. "She doesn't believe he died. She thinks he went on his own." Sort of a freelance spy.

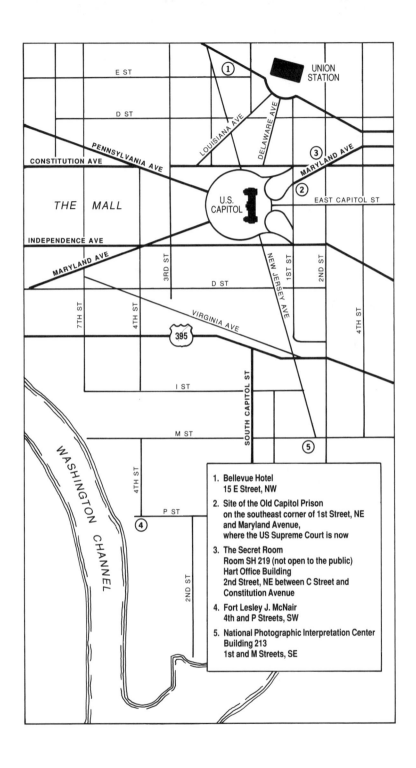

E ST

D ST

UNION STATION

LOUISIANA AVE

DELAWARE AVE

MARYLAND AVE

PENNSYLVANIA AVE

CONSTITUTION AVE

THE MALL

U.S. CAPITOL

EAST CAPITOL ST

INDEPENDENCE AVE

MARYLAND AVE

3RD ST

D ST

NEW JERSEY AVE

1ST ST

2ND ST

4TH ST

7TH ST

4TH ST

VIRGINIA AVE

395

I ST

SOUTH CAPITOL ST

M ST

WASHINGTON CHANNEL

4TH ST

P ST

2ND ST

1. Bellevue Hotel
    15 E Street, NW

2. Site of the Old Capitol Prison
    on the southeast corner of 1st Street, NE
    and Maryland Avenue,
    where the US Supreme Court is now

3. The Secret Room
    Room SH 219 (not open to the public)
    Hart Office Building
    2nd Street, NE between C Street and
    Constitution Avenue

4. Fort Lesley J. McNair
    4th and P Streets, SW

5. National Photographic Interpretation Center
    Building 213
    1st and M Streets, SE

And Then There Were None
Bellevue Hotel
15 E Street N.W.

Walter Krivitsky signed the register at the Bellevue Hotel on Capitol Hill at 5:49 P.M. on Sunday, February 9, 1941. When he got to Room 524, he ordered a bottle of soda. A bellboy took it up to him. The next morning, a chambermaid found him dead with a bullet hole in his right temple. The door to his room was locked. Although a window was open, police could see no way in from the outside. The coroner ruled it a suicide.

Even though there were three suicide notes, his friends didn't believe it. He wasn't depressed, and besides, he had made plans to buy a car. He was also about to assume a new identity and had taken steps to change his name. Was he, as they say in the spy business, sent to heaven? The victim of a wet affair? (A wet affair isn't a pool party; it's KGB tradecraft jargon for murder and assassination.)

Krivitsky had been the head of Soviet military intelligence for Western Europe. He had broken with Stalin in 1937, after the blood purge of senior officers of the Red Army. He was the only general to survive. In Paris at the time, he decided to find another line of work.

In interviews with British intelligence, he fingered a number of Soviet secret agents. Then, in America in 1939, he told a prescient tale—to a congressional committee and in articles for the *Saturday Evening Post*. He related how the OGPU (a predecessor to the KGB) tracked down Stalin's foes in foreign lands, kidnapping and murdering them if necessary. Krivitsky had reason to feel nervous.

Before the events at the hotel, Krivitsky had told his friends he was being followed and to be suspicious if anything happened to him. A verdict of suicide was compelling: The pistol was his. But some of his friends felt that, at the very least, he was hounded to death. Even the prosecutor didn't rule out the idea that, if it were suicide, it was coerced—a "Kremlin suicide," in which members of Stalin's inner circle, fallen from grace, killed themselves to spare their families' destruction by the OGPU.

Krivitsky had a wife and a seven-year-old son in New York City. In his note to his wife he wrote: "I want to live very badly, but it is impossible."

Reflecting on the case, one former CIA official said, "In counterintelligence business, there are no closed cases, and it doesn't really matter what people say about the event, it ain't proven. We don't know how he made his exit, and it may have been assisted."

As it says in the foreword to Krivitsky's memoirs, *In Stalin's Secret Service*, "Any fool can commit murder; it takes experience to commit a natural death."

Since then, the Bellevue Hotel hasn't changed much outside, with its plain red brick facade and green canopy. During recent renovations, the size of the rooms doubled and the Tiber Creek Pub replaced the cafeteria. The room that was Krivitsky's is rather plain—a desk, a dresser, a small bed with a quilted blue-flowered bedspread and a view of the Capitol between buildings.

"To be perfectly honest, it bears no resemblance to what its previous configuration was," said Paul Delaney, general manager. "Things back then looked far more lean in terms of decorative concept. The hotel would have been an overnight stop, the place where you stayed when you were waiting for trains."

Today the room rate is $99.50 plus tax, for single occupancy. Krivitsky paid $2.50. Room 524 is a popular one. When the American Latvian Society meets at the hotel every year, one or two members ask to stay in it. "That room has been asked for on a great number of occasions," Delaney said. "One scarcely dares imagine why. Lots of people like to attach themselves to morbid things like that. I scarcely dare speculate. . .unless someone is trying to get in touch with General Krivitsky."

The Rebel Press Agent
Site of the Old Capitol Prison
Corner of First Street N.E. and Maryland Avenue, where the U.S. Supreme Court is now

Belle Boyd's acclaim was exceeded only by her *réclame*. "The Rebel Spy" was her own best press agent, with a flair for the dramatic. She did her spying out in the Shenandoah Valley and soon came to Washington to pass some time in the Old Capitol Prison. The Federals could tolerate her spying but not her publicity and had set a trap for her.

Before her arrest, she had been an *agent provocateur*, in short a flirt, trying to draw out the Union officers. In her memoirs, she tells how, dressed in white sunbonnet, blue dress and white apron, she braved Union rifle fire to get a message to Stonewall Jackson as his divisions converged a few miles from Front Royal, Virginia. Jackson, she said, was "that undaunted hero, that true apostle of freedom." The Union army was "the spoiler."

She was no beauty, but she had style. A reporter at the *New York Daily Tribune* described her as having "a superb figure, an intellectual face" and dressing "with much taste. . .[She] wears a gold palmetto tree beneath her beautiful chin, a Rebel soldier's belt around her waist and a velvet band across her forehead, with 7 stars of the Confederacy shedding their pale light therefrom."

And sometimes she wore a revolver in her belt. She shot a Union officer once, at the age of 18, but she only wounded him, and, she confessed, she just did it because he had offended her mother.

She compared the Old Capitol Prison to the Bastille. The difference was that in a few months she would get out.

While walking in the prison yard, she supposedly sported a small Confederate flag in her bosom. Every evening she would sing, to the annoyance of the prison guards, the song known as the Marseillaise of the South, "Maryland, My Maryland." The border state had more mixed allegiance than most.

"Avenge the patriotic gore that flecked the streets of Baltimore," she sang. No doubt she crooned the closing lines lustily: "Hurrah!

Portrait of Belle Boyd, taken by Civil War photographer Mathew Brady.

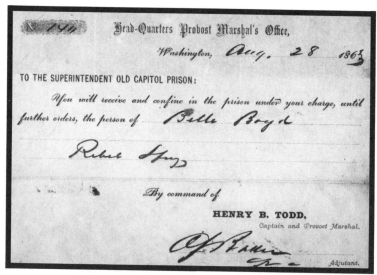

An order for the arrest of "Belle Boyd, Rebel Spy" is on file at the National Archives.

During the Civil War, the Old Capitol Prison was the jail for spies and Secessionists.

She spurns the Northern scum!/She breathes, she lives; she'll come, she'll come!/ Maryland! My Maryland!"All this practicing stood her in good stead, for five years later—after being sent South, traveling to England, marrying, becoming a mother and being widowed—*La Belle Rebelle* made her American stage debut in September 1867 in the St. Louis Grand Opera House. In her later years, she re-enacted that thrilling dramatic narrative, "North and South—or, The Perils of a Spy." Her most enthusiastic audiences turned out to be Union veterans.

The Secret Room
Room SH 219 (not open to the public), Hart Office Building
Second Street N.E. between C Street and Constitution Avenue

Up on Capitol Hill you may hear more than one apocryphal tale. One tall story has it that John Quincy Adams, when he was a member of the House of Representatives, eavesdropped on the opposition in the Old House Chamber by virtue of the shape of the room. With its curved ceiling, the chamber was and is notorious for strange acoustics. During the 47 years the House met there, the members tried to get better acoustics so that the speaker could be heard from the podium, at least. The eavesdropping myth falls flat when you consider that everyone knew that their whispers could be heard on the other side of the chamber. So it's likely that house members left the room to brew strategy.

Quite the opposite of that chamber—the ultimate deterrent to eavesdropping on the Hill—is found behind an unmarked door in the Hart Office Building in suite SH 219.

An opaque glass door opens into a carpeted foyer guarded by a member of the Capitol police. Only members or staff of the Senate Select Committee on Intelligence, whose offices are down the corridor and around a corner, may go any farther. Any visitors they bring must sign in, at a curved desk in an alcove a little like a coat check. Instead of leaving coats, they prepare to shed their secrets.

Inside, SH 219 is one of the most secure installations in the government: a bug-proof, sound-proof chamber that would give the wiliest KGB bugging expert a run for his rubles. Protected by vaulted doors, it is a room within a room, raised so that the walls can be inspected routinely for bugs. The room's steel casing prevents any electromagnetic waves from entering or leaving. Even the electrical supply is filtered electronically to prevent any signal emanations.

The inner room is divided into smaller rooms. In these inner chambers, CIA and NSA briefers drop their secrets like so much heavy baggage. There is also a hearing room where the senators take closed testimony. But here, alas, technology breaks down.

The witness desk is outfitted with a PA system. Reminiscent of John Quincy Adams days, it was not able to make the muttering of William J. Casey audible. In fact, the joke around town was that the CIA director mumbled so badly he didn't need a scrambler phone.

Just for him, the committee installed a separate system, which allowed senators to plug in earphones and turn up the volume. Interestingly enough, that did no good. Those who knew him say Casey was perfectly understandable—but only when he wanted to be heard. The Casey system is no longer used.

The Downing File
Fort Lesley J. McNair
Fourth and P Streets, S.W.

Fort McNair, a manicured finger of land that reaches into the mouth of the Anacostia River, is home to the National War College, where soldiers from all over the world go to study global strategies. During its 200-year history, the base has served as an arsenal, a penitentiary and a hospital. Among its more notorious visitors, the military garrison saw the Lincoln conspirators and a little-known Spanish-American War spy, George Downing.

In May 1898, Downing was a prisoner in the former guard house, a tan building with brown trim, now somewhat hidden from view behind the base's tennis courts. Fort McNair was then called Washington Barracks. There in the guard house a few days after his arrest, in his cell which was actually a cage, the morose young man tore a towel in half and tied a silk handkerchief to it. He made a noose and hanged himself from the steel bars over his head.

Downing's career as a spy had been a short one. He had served as a petty officer aboard the U.S. Navy ship *Brooklyn*. In Washington he stayed in a boarding house at 916 E Street N.W. (in the same block as FBI headquarters now), and, according to the *Evening Star* accounts, had fallen in love with a woman at the Spanish legation: "She evidently made him the instrument by which he could become most useful to the Spanish government. It is not believed she felt the least affection for him."

The mysterious dark-haired woman put him in touch with Spanish intelligence chief Lieutenant Ramon Carranza, the former Washington naval attaché. When Downing went to visit him in Toronto, Carranza himself was already under surveillance. The U.S. Secret Service followed the recruit back to Washington. Downing stopped by the Navy Department, learned what he could and wrote it up in a letter to a contact in Montreal. He mailed the letter at the main post office, Pennsylvania Avenue and 12th Street N.W. Secret Service agents who were tailing him intercepted the letter and found more incriminating papers in his room. Downing was arrested and taken to the Washington Barracks. Apparently, the evidence was overwhelming, even to Downing. The old guard house is now the chaplain's quarters. There has been talk of converting the house into a golf shack for the benefit of the base's popular seven-hole golf course.

Just next door, Building 21 is all that remains of America's first federal penitentiary—officers' quarters. Here in the former east wing, Lincoln conspirators Mary Surratt, George Atzerodt, David Herold and Lewis Powell (a.k.a. Paine) were tried and found guilty in the third floor courtroom. Occupants of the "Surratt House," as well as plumbers and electricians, have noted some strange goings-on in this building—doors locking behind them, lights turning themselves back on, a woman crying at night. It is said that there is always condensation on the window where Mary Surratt stood awaiting

The building that is the chaplain's quarters at Fort McNair looks the same now as it did during George Downing's day, when it was the Washington Barracks' guard house.

her execution. Tears? Apparently she plans to roam the area until her name is cleared.

The execution by hanging took place July 7, 1865. The gallows and the conspirators' temporary graves were just east of where the tennis courts are now, near the old Guard House, built after the penitentiary was torn down. The conspirators' bodies were released to their families four years later. So was the body of the ringleader, John Wilkes Booth. His temporary grave was under the floor of the penitentiary's center cell block, in front of the present Building 14, one of the officers' homes that line the broad greensward of Fort McNair. Booth is now buried in Baltimore's Green Mount Cemetery, and Surratt in Mount Olivet Cemetery in Northeast Washington.

Out of Sight, Out of Mind
National Photographic Interpretation Center
Building 213, First and M Streets S.E.

They're tearing up M Street here, been doing it for years. With construction workers waving trucks every which way and no traffic signals, you just want to find your way back to a smooth strip of road. So you don't notice the *trompe-l'oeil* facade just to the right of the intersection. It looks like a derelict public school building, maybe a warehouse. But if you wend your way through the graveyard of GSA garages and warehouses here next to the Navy Yard, the illusion is shattered.

Chain-link fence topped with triple barbed wire surrounds Building 213—three massive impenetrable white cubes that house NPIC (pronounced EN-pick). An aggressive-looking security guard eyeballs every car that passes. On the roof, rotating security cameras take in everything he misses. Where there are windows, they vibrate—to foil eavesdroppers using laser beams. Some windows are simply bricked in.

At the old NPIC location in the Steuart Ford Building at Fifth and K (see page 52), analysts scrutinized photographs. A few miles but a quantum leap away, supercomputers now scan an endless stream of incoming imagery. If the computer finds a difference between the new and the known, an alarm sounds. So sophisticated is the system that it can tell from an image of smoke rising over a smokestack what has been burning. NPIC forecasts floods and estimates oil spills. And on July 23, 1990, it pinpointed the movement of Iraqi troops toward Kuwait. Once, a *Washington Post* reporter entered the building on his own and got as far as the cafeteria. Using his Pentagon pass, he got to the elevator and took it to the cafeteria, where he called a source for an interview.

"How about a tour of the building? I'm down here in the cafeteria."

Nice try.

Pretty clever of the CIA to locate such a sensitive facility in a rundown neighborhood where abandoned sofas dot the front yards and craters pock the roads. A totally anonymous building, known by a number, not a name. There's a small slip, though, in the towing-enforced parking lot, where each spot is marked reserved for NPIC.

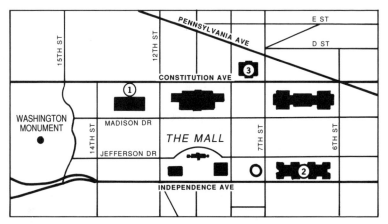

1. National Museum of American History
   Constitution Avenue between 12th and
   14th Streets, NW

2. National Air and Space Museum
   6th Street and Independence Avenue, SW

3. National Archives
   Pennsylvania Avenue at 8th Street, NW

The Kremlin, Magic and the On-the-Roof Gang

Sites at the west end of Constitution Avenue N.W. and along Ohio Drive

During World War II and for a few years after, much of the federal government's activity in divining other governments' secrets took place in the Mall area. Broad stretches of green along Constitution Avenue and around the Reflecting Pool, the oldtimers will tell you, used to be the sites of a number of temporary buildings. Built during the war, these ramshackle, low slung "tempos" housed the government overflow. Before the CIA moved to Langley in 1961, it had offices in three, two-story tempos in West Potomac Park on Ohio Drive along the river, in quonset huts on the south side of the Reflecting Pool and in tempos at the west end of Constitution Avenue. Some of the buildings were so rickety that safes for holding classified documents routinely came crashing through the upper floors to land near startled people below.

The agency's predecessor, the OSS, had had its headquarters in a more substantial complex of yellow brick buildings that sit on a little hill at the foot of E Street, along 23rd Street. This off-limits complex is now known as the Navy Department's Bureau of Medicine and Surgery, but it still has some CIA offices. During World War II, a building there that housed the OSS, 2430 E Street N.W., was known as "The Kremlin." OSS founder "Wild Bill" Donovan occupied a corner office on the first floor. On the west side, near where Kennedy Center is now, the complex overlooked the Heurich Brewery and Riverside Stadium, a roller rink. Before it was razed, the roller rink slowed down considerably: It was converted to a library and file-storage area for the agency.

Along the south side of Constitution Avenue there were also two large, three-story tempos built during World War I. One, the

71

WAR DEPARTMENT
WAR DEPARTMENT GENERAL STAFF BY AUTHORITY OF A. C. OF S., WPD
WAR PLANS DIVISION
WASHINGTON   *12/7/41.* ....*CRC.7*........
                          Date   *Initials*

December 7, 1941.

MEMORANDUM FOR THE ADJUTANT GENERAL (Through Secretary, General Staff)

      Subject: Far East Situation.

          The Secretary of War directs that the following first priority secret radiogram be sent to the Commanding General, U.S. Army Forces in the Far East; Commanding General, Carribean Defense Command; Commanding General, Hawaiian Department; Commanding General, Fourth Army:

          Japanese are presenting at one p.m. Eastern Standard time today what amounts to an ultimatum also they are under orders to destroy their Code machine immediately stop Just what significance the hour set may have we do not know but be on alert accordingly stop Inform naval authorities of this communication.

                   MARSHALL

O.C.S.
12/7/41 Jeu

                      L. T. GEROW,
                 Brigadier General,
        Acting Assistant Chief of Staff.

Code messages
Sent out
Dec. → Radios as follows dispatched 11:52 AM, 12-7-41,
          by Code Room, WDMC:
     12.05 ' #733 to CG, USAFFE, Manila, P.I.;
     12.17 ' #529 to CG, Haw. Dept., Ft. Shafter. TH.
     12.00 ' #519 to CG, Crbn. Def. Cmnd., Quarry Heights, CZ
     12:11 ' #16 to CG, Fourth Army, Pres. of San Fco., Cal.
             ehb - 1705.

REGRADE
ORDER SEC AK(m)
BY TAG PEN
9 d 5

UNCLASSIFIED

FILE JAN -3 1942

When this first priority secret radiogram was transmitted, the attack on Pearl Harbor was still a few hours away.

old Main Navy Building at 17th and Constitution Avenue, had an unusual structure jutting from the roof. It was a steel-reinforced concrete blockhouse where from 1926 to 1941 Navy and Marine Corps radio operators got special sound-proofed training in headsets and handkeys. After a few months of rooftop classes, the intercept operators would go on to the Pacific Theater to try their hand at intercepting the real thing—naval and diplomatic communications. They called themselves the On-the-Roof Gang.

Next door at 19th and Constitution, in what was then the Munitions Building, the Japanese diplomatic cipher, PURPLE, was broken in September 1939 by the Signal Intelligence Service. In offices on the third floor, head cryptanalyst William Friedman and his group reconstructed the PURPLE cipher machine the Japanese were using—just as the British and the Poles had done with Germany's ENIGMA. Translations of such decrypted Japanese communications were codenamed MAGIC, and the daily reports of them, MAGIC summaries. Because the cipher had been broken, American officials read Japan's final communication to the Japanese embassy in Washington hours before the attack on Pearl Harbor. Deciphered in the Main Navy Building, the Japanese message bore instructions to embassy personnel to destroy their cipher machine and to deliver an ultimatum. But from the communications they'd been seeing, the Americans didn't piece together what was happening. Even MAGIC wasn't magical enough.

By sheer coincidence, in 1942 both signal intelligence operations moved from the two large tempos to former girls' schools—the SIS to Arlington Hall, and the Navy's Communications Security Group to 3801 Nebraska Avenue N.W., where it evolved into the Naval Security Group. Cryptologic work expands to fill the space allowed for it.

Learning to Love the Bombe
National Museum of American History
Constitution Avenue between 12th and 14th Streets N.W.

T he elephant in the rotunda of the
Natural History Museum has probably served as brush-contact point
and drop site countless times. We'll never know. But the Smithsonian
Institution relates to espionage mainly in the traditional ways. The
forensic people routinely work with the FBI, examining old bones
and so forth. And, of course, some of the museums collect the objects
that once briefly held the power of talismans—memorabilia of spy-
dom that sometimes bubble up from the secret depths.

The CIA's Historical Intelligence Collection hides from public
view at headquarters, while NSA insists that it has no museum, just
a lot of artifacts. Fortunately, NSA has made a long-term loan of
objects from its cryptologic cache to the National Museum of American History. These can be seen in the Timekeeping Hall at least
until 1992, when that hall will be moved, and in a permanent ex-
hibition, "Information Age: People, Information and Technology."

During World War II, the ingenious Enigma machine was used
by German armed forces, from Hitler on down, to encipher messages.
Germany's unfounded confidence in the system's invulnerability became a major advantage to the Allies, who were able to duplicate
the machines.

Actually, they look a lot like old Underwood portable type-
writers. But with Enigma, each key the soldier would hit on the
keyboard enciphered a character of the message he wished to send.
While the three-rotor one could encipher $26 \times 26 \times 26$ characters
(that's 17,576), more sophisticated versions could generate more
than 100 trillion cipher combinations. No wonder Hitler felt secure.

The *bombe* was the high-speed calculating machine the Allies
used to determine the most likely settings the Enigma operator had
used for his message; it simulated 16 four-rotor Enigmas at once.
Then, as if they were the intended recipients of the message, crypt-
analysts used the projected settings on their own rip-off version

National Museum of American History

America's answer to the German Enigma machine (pictured in foreground) was the massive gizmo called the bombe. *They are displayed together in the "Information Age" gallery at the National Museum of American History.*

Enigma machines to solve the cipher. One of these *bombes* is displayed in the "Information Age" gallery. A large gray cabinet the size of a van, with a mass of wires and wheels, it resembles an old-fashioned Univac computer. Secrets were its currency, and the National Cash Register Company built it.

"Information Age" also has a fingers-on display that tells how the FBI automatic fingerprint-reader system works, as well as a small display of gadgets left over from Watergate. The microphones and transmitter for bugging the Democratic National Committee head-quarters in 1972 are disguised as Chapsticks (two, wired, watch your lips) and a smoke detector with gummed labels. In retrospect, it's hard to imagine the labels fooling anyone with their superfluous message: "Fire Equipment, Do Not Move."

A cipher device used by Pancho Villa c. 1914 and a compass used by Lewis and Clark are included in the collection, but are not on display. Initially, the mission of Captain Meriwether Lewis and Lieutenant William Clark was styled as a covert military intelligence operation. Using false identities, they were to scout out the land and its people beyond the Mississippi and to discover where best to build fortifications. The assignment came right from the top—Thomas Jefferson, one of several spymaster-presidents this country has had. But the Louisiana Purchase of 1803 from the Mississippi to the Rockies changed their secret mission into an innocent surveying job.

Mystery Ships
National Air and Space Museum
Sixth Street and Independence Avenue S.W.

Visitors to the "Looking at Earth" gallery enjoy punching in a map of their hometown as seen by a Landsat satellite. Displayed among the benign weather satellites in the "Looking at Earth" gallery are two reconnaissance planes used

National Air and Space Museum

The first U-2 reconnaissance plane to overfly Russia is exhibited in the National Air and Space Museum.

in war and peace. One, a deHavilland DH-4, was used for aerial reconnaissance during World War I. The other is a Lockheed U-2, designed for high-altitude photo reconnaissance in the mid-1950s. This particular plane actually overflew Russia, aggravating the Soviets because they couldn't do anything about it. Then, when they developed the missile technology, the Soviets shot down Francis Gary Powers's U-2 on a strategic reconnaissance mission over Sverdlovsk in May 1960. Powers was a former Air Force pilot who had gone to work for the CIA as a civilian. (See page 114.)

The museum owns a Lockheed SR-71 Blackbird, the successor to the U-2. At the moment, this sleek mystery ship is grounded at Dulles along with a space shuttle, awaiting the launch of an Air and Space Annex for the really big planes. Looking like a dark prototype for a Darth Vader ship, the Blackbird flew its last mission in 1990. The Blackbird wasn't considered cost-effective. At the time, it was the fastest plane ever flown from a runway. Cruising speed: Mach 3 plus.

They Never Forget a Spy
National Archives
Pennsylvania Avenue at Eighth Street N.W.

On the south side of the National Archives, tourist-pilgrims line up in shorts and Hard Rock Cafe T-shirts to pay homage to the Declaration of Independence, the Constitution and the Bill of Rights. On the north side, researchers in shirts open at the collar, crumpled pants or faded skirts file in to view other more obscure documents in the federal record.

Here in the Archives—the national memory—spying in America has left a paper trail. A few of its Greatest Hits: the OSS Archives; NSA and CIA histories; the records of the Military Intelligence Division of the War Department; the Pumpkin Papers, on microfilm. New releases: the records of the Manhattan Project, and The Nixon

An excerpt from a transcript of the Nixon White House Tapes. These Watergate tapes are available for public listening at the National Archives' Nixon Project.

Tapes, I and II, most of them made in the Oval Office. Part II came out in June 1991.

Among the miles of files, researchers can request the reports of investigations on Charlie Chaplin, Margaret Mead, and Helen Keller, among others. Whether they were suspected of subversion

```
PRESIDENT:     Oh, I know.  But I suggested that the other day and we
               all came down on, uh, remember we came down on, uh, on
               the negative on it.  Now what's changed our mind?

DEAN:          The lack of alternatives or a body.

               [Laughter]

EHRLICHMAN:    We, we went down every alley.  [Laughter] Let it go over.

PRESIDENT:     Well, I feel that at, uh, I feel that this is, that,
               uh, I feel that at the very minimum we've got to have the
               statement and, uh, let's look at it, whatever the hell it
               is.  If, uh, if it opens up doors, it opens up doors,
               you know.

EHRLICHMAN:    John says he's sorry he sent those burglars in there,
               and that helps a lot.

PRESIDENT:     That's right.

MITCHELL:      You are very welcome, sir.

               [Laughter]

HALDEMAN:      Just glad the others didn't get caught.

PRESIDENT:     Yeah, the ones we sent to Muskie and all the rest; Jackson,
               and Hubert, and, uh [unintelligible]


                              -85-
```

or just people applying for government jobs, they're all filed together now.

There are 65 boxes of German U-boat intercepts and 16 boxes of Magic summaries: the gist of decrypted World War II Japanese diplomatic messages put together for top officials so they could quickly scan whatever was coming in.

Helping researchers wade their way through all this are archivists like John E. Taylor, keeper of the paper kingdom, 45 years on the job, who likes to thumb through the records and often will randomly open a box only to discover inside the answer to a researcher's question that has long been lying on his desk. Best-selling espionage authors call him their "secret weapon."

Through the mail you can purchase such spy memorabilia as the Turner-Baker papers (on microfilm), which were concerned with dubious dealings from the Union viewpoint during the Civil War. From select audiovisual records, you can order copies of broadcast summaries of the proceedings of the House Un-American Activities Committee, including testimony from confessed spy Elizabeth Bentley, alleged spy Alger Hiss and FBI informant Ronald Reagan, as well as broadcast interviews of Senator Joseph McCarthy (R-Wisconsin) babbling about his exposure of "Communists" and "crooks." You can also order a photo, suitable for framing, of the Federal observation balloon *Intrepid* being inflated in May 1862 for the Battle of Fair Oaks, Virginia.

DEAN: Yes.

PRESIDENT: Then he can go over there as soon [unintelligible] this. But,
             uh, the, uh, the one thing I don't want to do is to --
             Now let me make this clear. I, I, I thought it was, uh,
             very, uh, very cruel thing as it turned out -- although
             at the time I had to tell [unintelligible] -- what
             happened to Adams. I don't want it to happen with
             Watergate -- the Watergate matter. I think he made a,
             made a mistake, but he shouldn't have been sacked, he
             shouldn't have been -- And, uh, for that reason, I am
             perfectly willing to -- I don't give a shit what
             happens. I want you all to stonewall it, let them
             plead the Fifth Amendment, cover-up or anything else,
             if it'll save it -- save the plan. That's the whole
             point. On the other hand, uh, uh, I would prefer, as
             I said to you, that you do it the other way. And I
             would particularly prefer to do it that other way if
             it's going to come out that way anyway. And that my
             view, that, uh, with the number of jackass people that
             they've got that they can call, they're going to -- The
             story they get out through leaks, charges, and so forth,
             and innuendos, will be a hell of a lot worse than the
             story they're going to get out by just letting it
             out there.

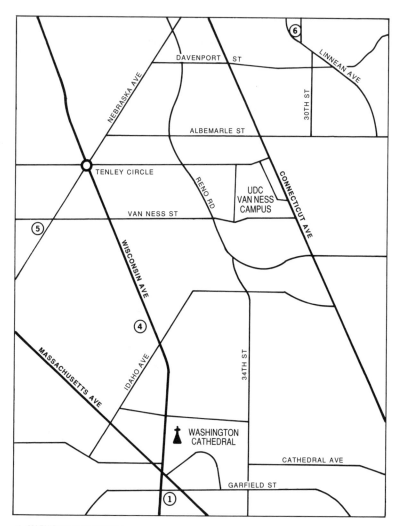

1. **MARY'S apartment building**
   at 2800 Wisconsin Avenue, NW
2. **Former Soviet Military Office (SMO)**
   2552 Belmont Road, NW
3. **Residence of the French Ambassador**
   2221 Kalorama Road, NW
   formerly the Vichy French Mission
4. **McLean Gardens**
   Wisconsin Avenue at Porter, Rodman
   and Newark Streets, NW
5. **Former home of Harold "Kim" Philby**
   4100 Nebraska Avenue, NW
6. **J. Edgar Hoover's residence**
   4936 30th Place, NW

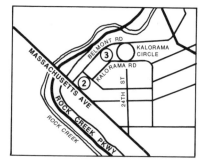

Codename MARY
Apartment building at 2800 Wisconsin Avenue N.W.

The KGB has a name for her: swallow. The swallow's nest is her apartment, usually equipped with cameras and recorders. Her male counterpart is the raven. The FBI has its own word for operations that lure foreign agents into compromising positions: honey pot.

But Jennifer Miles, the sexy spy for Cuba, was no Mata Hari. She was just a very pretty secretary at the South African Embassy who went on vacation to Cuba in 1968. While there she became impressed with the goals of the Cuban Revolution. The Cuban intelligence service (the DGI) recruited her to work in Washington. Her codename was MARY.

Her method was simple. She slept with as many State Department, Defense Department and White House aides as she could. The FBI started watching her after a man trimming bushes in Jackson Heights, New York, discovered a report she had left for her handlers in a crack in a wall. The FBI was impressed enough to keep an eye on her for a year. At 2800 Wisconsin Avenue, they bugged her studio apartment, which was on the ground floor and conveniently had a picture window.

The agents stopped counting when the number of her beaus exceeded a hundred. They drew the line when she started dating White House aides to learn what she could from them. When confronted, Miles confessed. She was allowed to go home to South Africa so long as she agreed never to return to the United States.

The Dangle
Former Soviet Military Office (SMO)
2552 Belmont Road N.W.

Known in the trade as SMO, the former Soviet Military Office is a large red brick home sitting on a corner of Embassy Row. With its black shutters closed, the building looks like a haunted house. It tries to remain anonymous and unnoticed, except for the plaque by the door with the Russian words on it. Funny how people wanting to sell secrets to the Soviets could still find the place.

That was exactly the problem confronting FBI agent William P. O'Keefe in the spring of 1982. A member of the counterintelligence squad CI-3, based at the Washington Metropolitan Field Office at Buzzard Point, O'Keefe decided to catch the Soviets at their own game. If the Soviets got burned, it might discourage them from

Ronald Kessler

The former Soviet Military Office on Belmont Road, N.W., where some FBI counterintelligence agents have spent more time than they do at home.

dealing with just anybody who came in off the street. After calling around to Washington think-tanks looking for someone with a convincing profile, he found the perfect "dangle," or bait, in John L. Stine. First, as security officer for a defense research firm, Stine had access to classified material. But more than that, his lifestyle seemed to fit. He was a 40-year-old bachelor who frequented singles bars, drank Scotch and water even at lunchtime and chain-smoked Kools.

In a room in the Key Bridge Marriott, O'Keefe gave him a crash course on being a double agent. On Thanksgiving Day, the only holiday most Americans can agree on celebrating, Stine walked in to SMO. All he needed was a cover story about owing money to a bookie to persuade Vyacheslav Pavlov, a GRU officer, that he was genuine. Pavlov was pleased with the bogus classified documents Stine hauled out from under his sweater. When Stine was leaving SMO, Pavlov solicitously offered him a ride—in the trunk of his car.

After driving around to "dryclean" himself of any possible tail, Pavlov dropped the terrified Stine off on Connecticut Avenue. Stine hailed a cab back to the Marriott, where, in the parking lot where

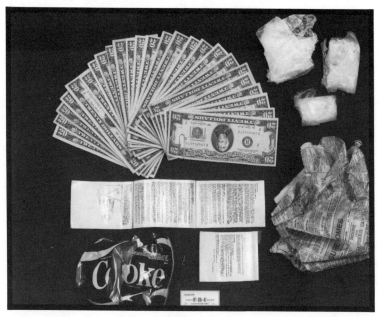

Evidence from the FBI sting "Operation Jagwire" which resulted in two GRU officers' returning to the Soviet Union.

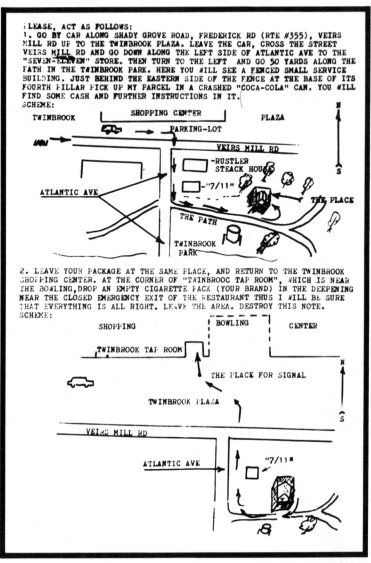

; LEASE, ACT AS FOLLOWS:

1. GO BY CAR ALONG SHADY GROVE ROAD, FREDERICK RD (RTE #355), VEIRS MILL RD UP TO THE TWINBROOK PLAZA. LEAVE THE CAR, CROSS THE STREET VEIRS MILL RD AND GO DOWN ALONG THE LEFT SIDE OF ATLANTIC AVE TO THE "SEVEN-ELEVEN" STORE. THEN TURN TO THE LEFT AND GO 50 YARDS ALONG THE PATH IN THE TWINBROOK PARK. HERE YOU WILL SEE A FENCED SMALL SERVICE BUILDING. JUST BEHIND THE EASTERN SIDE OF THE FENCE AT THE BASE OF ITS FOURTH PILLAR PICK UP MY PARCEL IN A CRASHED "COCA-COLA" CAN. YOU WILL FIND SOME CASH AND FURTHER INSTRUCTIONS IN IT.

SCHEME:

2. LEAVE YOUR PACKAGE AT THE SAME PLACE, AND RETURN TO THE TWINBROOK SHOPPING CENTER. AT THE CORNER OF "TWINBROOC TAP ROOM", WHICH IS NEAR THE BOWLING, DROP AN EMPTY CIGARETTE PACK (YOUR BRAND) IN THE DEEPENING NEAR THE CLOSED EMERGENCY EXIT OF THE RESTAURANT THUS I WILL BE SURE THAT EVERYTHING IS ALL RIGHT. LEAVE THE AREA. DESTROY THIS NOTE.

SCHEME:

Federal Bureau of Investigation

In this set of instructions, GRU officer Vyacheslav Pavlov tells a double agent to leave documents in Twinbrook Park, where he will also find his cash payment in a "crashed" Coke can.

he had left his car, he signaled O'Keefe that all was well, by placing his Irish walking hat on the car's roof.

In the following months, the charade known as Operation Jagwire continued. In his one-time-only performance as a double agent, Stine found himself searching in the snow for cigarette packs full of instructions and crawling on his knees to look for crushed Coke cans containing money. In a note left for Stine in a Coke can near Twinbrook Shopping Center in Rockville, Pavlov told him how to photograph "highest classification docs." He warned him to buy the rolls of film at different stores. (Stine didn't take the pictures; an FBI photographer did, purposely muffing a few frames to make it look like Stine's work.) Stine was to wrap the undeveloped rolls in a black plastic garbage bag and drop them at the base of a gnarled tree at the intersection of Schaeffer Road and White Ground Road in Boyds, Maryland.

On the night of April 16, 1983, special agents waiting near the gnarled tree got an unexpected bonus. Retrieving the bogus documents was someone the SMO-watchers instantly recognized: Soviet Army Lieutenant Colonel Yevgeniy Barmyantsev, the acting military attaché at SMO and Pavlov's boss. The agents didn't arrest him. When Barmyantsev cried, "I am diplomat!" they knew it all too well. Instead, two days later, the State Department declared him *persona non grata*.

As a result of Operation Jagwire, both diplomats were recalled to Moscow. But the Cold-War game wasn't over. The counterintelligence squad played the role of the sorcerer's apprentice—for every one they knocked out, two more seemed to appear.

A Local Mata Hari
Residence of the French Ambassador
2221 Kalorama Road N.W., formerly the Vichy French mission

Her codename was CYNTHIA. In 1940, the patriotic seductress who also called herself Elizabeth

Thorpe lived in a rented house in Georgetown, at 3327 O Street N.W. To be near her lover, she later took a room at the Wardman Park (now the Sheraton-Washington's Wardman Towers, Connecticut Avenue and Woodley Road N.W.). But she did some of her best work on her back at the Vichy French mission.

"I discovered how easy it was to make highly trained, professionally close-mouthed patriots give away secrets in bed," she wrote. "The greatest joy is a man and a woman together. Making love allows a discharge of all those private innermost thoughts that have accumulated. In this sudden flood everything is released," she noted, according to William Stevenson's *A Man Called Intrepid*.

Anything for the cause. As British Security Coordination described her in its papers, "A woman agent under the direction of BSC in New York accomplished the most important work that opened the way back into France and ultimately into Germany. She had a soft soothing voice which doubtless in itself inspired confidences. Her appeal to her victims was in the first place intellectual. The discovery of her physical attraction came later, as an intoxicating realization."

Although Cynthia worked for the British, she had been born in Minneapolis, daughter of a Marine Corps major and granddaughter of a Minnesota state senator. She had gotten her start as a Mata Hari in 1937 in Poland. "Bored" with her diplomat husband Arthur Pack, she took on influential lovers in Warsaw. Fortunately for the eventual solution of the ULTRA secret, Cynthia possessed an understanding husband.

She was sent to Washington to work on Italian and Vichy French diplomats. One of her conquests when she was in Paris before World War II had been an admiral who was now the Italian naval attaché in Washington. Blindly, he passed on the Italian naval ciphers. Quickly, she dropped him.

In 1940, William S. Stephenson, chief of BSC, visited her in her Georgetown house, meeting with her in the library facing on O Street. He called himself Mr. Williams, but she knew him to be INTREPID. Her impossible mission, which she decided to accept, was to gather for the Allies all letters and cables between the Vichy French in Washington and Europe.

To that end, she commenced an affair with Captain Charles Brousse, a former naval fighter pilot who was press officer to Vichy Ambassador Gaston Henri-Haye. In 1941, for the sake of conve-

During the Second World War, the French ambassador's residence was the Vichy French embassy, where CYNTHIA did her best work.

nience, she moved into a room at the Wardman Park Hotel, where Brousse lived with his wife. Her specific assignment in March 1942 was to steal the new Vichy French naval cryptosystem from a safe in the embassy code room.

Brousse, a Frenchman of understandably confused loyalties, brought her into the elegant English Renaissance-style mansion on Kalorama Road. The guards winked at the couple's obvious need to be alone. Their several nights of making love on a sofa climaxed in failed attempts at stealing the ciphers. But, after a few visits from a visiting-fireman safecracker, Cynthia succeeded in spiriting the cipher books to a BSC man waiting outside the embassy, who returned the books five hours later. From Washington, Cynthia went to Canada, where she was trained as an assassin. Stephenson persuaded her to start a career in research instead. Not quite the equivalent of taking up knitting but almost as safe.

G-Girl
McLean Gardens
Wisconsin Avenue at Porter, Rodman and Newark Streets N.W.

On March 4, 1949, Judith Coplon, 27, Barnard graduate in requisite pullover sweater and pearls, was walking down a street in Manhattan with a friend when FBI agents came up and arrested them both. Coplon was a political analyst in the foreign agents registration section in the Justice Department in Washington. Her friend was Valentin Gubitchev, 32, a Russian engineer on the United Nations staff.

Fear of the "Red Peril" was high, but it was clear that here was a solid case of trafficking in national secrets. In her purse, agents found typewritten summaries of FBI internal security reports—including a decoy memo that the FBI had asked her boss to show her.

More evidence was discovered in her apartment in Jefferson Hall at McLean Gardens, 3685 38th Street N.W. Originally, the McLean

The fountain at McLean Gardens, where spy Judith Coplon lived in 1949. The sculpture was part of a much more elaborate fountain at the original McLean estate where the apartment complex was built.

Gardens complex was built in 1942 to house people coming to Washington to work in the war effort. In Coplon's day it continued to be a popular residence for single women who worked for the government ("G-girls," of which more later), as it was conveniently located on a bus line. Since then, a section of the original complex—including the residence hall where Coplon lived—has been razed and replaced by tony townhouses. Before moving to McLean Gardens, she had lived in a one-room apartment at 2634 Tunlaw N.W., a three-story red brick building still in existence.

According to the *Evening Star*, her fellow residents remembered her as studious, quiet, and "unusually fond of music." In fact, the only complaint her landlord had about her was that she sometimes typed until two o'clock in the morning. Xerox had not been invented, of course. Coplon had taken home reams of documents and typed out copies for Gubitchev, the Russian spy.

"Val," she testified at the first of her two trials, was the only man she truly loved—although he was married. Things really heated up in court, however, when the prosecution accused her of also having an affair with a Justice aide in the criminal division. Looking over at her recently widowed mother, Coplon angrily denied it.

Pamela Kessler

The logo on the stone wall at McLean Gardens, where spy Judith Coplon was one of the "government girls" living in Jefferson Hall in 1949.

In the courtroom she screamed at her lawyer: "You son of a bitch! I told you this would happen. How could you let it happen with my mother in the courtroom?" Finally, she did admit that she had spent some time alone with the Justice aide, in hotels and at his apartment.

She admitted, too, that she had taken extracts of secret FBI reports but had had no intention of showing them to the Russians. Indeed, she needed the papers for a novel she was writing—*Government Girl*.

She was convicted, but it didn't stick. The FBI hadn't quite worked out some sticky questions. At the time, a warrant was required for an espionage arrest, and they hadn't had one. And the court ruled that the government failed to prove that the FBI did not use evidence from illegal wiretaps. Gubitchev was shipped back to Russia. Coplon married Albert Socolov, a lawyer with the firm that handled her defense, and settled down to become a housewife and mother of four.

The Third Man, a Legend
Former home of Harold "Kim" Philby
4100 Nebraska Avenue N.W.

In 1951, while assigned to the British Embassy as First Secretary and CIA liaison man, Harold "Kim" Philby lived in the large neoclassical tan brick house at 4100 Nebraska Avenue N.W. His career as an agent for the Soviets lasted more than 20 years, but its turning point came at this house.

Involved were two of his friends, the infamous Burgess and Maclean from Cambridge in the thirties, where they had all joined the political left. At one time or another, all three were moles in the British embassy, at 3100 Massachusetts Avenue N.W. Donald Maclean, as First Secretary starting in 1944, had had access, through the Atomic Energy Commission, to the Americans' nuclear bomb planning. He was passing on the information. By 1949, the Soviets knew

The once and former home of Soviet ace of spies Kim Philby still stands on Nebraska Avenue.

that their agent Maclean—codenamed HOMER—was under suspicion. But their hunger for secrets exceeded their concern. Maclean's drinking problem worsened; he was moved to a diplomatic post back in London.

Meanwhile, Guy Burgess went to the embassy in Washington to work on Far Eastern affairs in 1950. A flamboyant homosexual and an alcoholic, he was not exactly welcomed by Philby's wife to the house on Nebraska Avenue. But he stayed there, until their Russian control decided it was time to warn Maclean. On a stroll in the garden behind the house one day, Philby talked to Burgess about warning Maclean back in London. The only problem was getting Burgess there. Burgess would have to get himself recalled. To do this, he would just have to be his incompetent self—only more so.

In March 1951, on a diplomatic speech-giving mission, Burgess managed to get himself stopped three times in Virginia for speeding; drunk, he boisterously threatened to invoke diplomatic immunity. He was brought home to London in short order. Then in May, Burgess headed off for Moscow with Maclean. The irony is that initially Burgess's departure may have been unintentional; he just hopped on a boat, and one thing led to another. He died an unhappy drunk in Moscow. Maclean may have done a little better as a Russian colonel.

When both men had fled to Russia, suspicion fell on Philby. He was recalled to England a month later for interrogation and was named in Parliament as the "third man" in the case. Still nothing happened to him. Much later, in Beirut in 1963, Philby began to sense that evidence was finally accumulating against him. Expected at a dinner party one night, he never arrived. He turned up in Moscow instead. He lived out his life quietly as a KGB general. In his lonely last years, even the KGB lost interest in him.

Hoover Slept Here
4936 30th Place N.W. and site at
413 Seward Square N.W.

While J. Edgar Hoover was The Director, he lived in a large colonial brick house with a slate roof, not far from Rock Creek Park. It was just a few miles across town from where he was born—in a muddy section of row houses called Pipetown, which had been occupied mostly by government workers and their families. His birthplace was a small stucco house at 413 Seward Square N.W., where a Methodist church stands now.

His home on 30th Place was stuffed with mementos. Souvenir photos of Hoover standing next to someone famous covered every inch of wall in the living room. In the event that the walls needed painting, the FBI kept diagrams so that the hundreds of photos could be rehung exactly where Hoover wanted them.

He was the talk of the neighborhood. The local gossip was that he had a tunnel built for quick exits.

"It's news to me," says Emily Spitzer, who lives there now with her husband, Joel Guiterman. "I would love to find something like that. In the course of renovation, we were hoping we'd find Jimmy Hoffa."

The only unusual thing they found was Astroturf—spread out like a warm breakfast all over the back yard and the lawn and on the

J. Edgar Hoover's rec room in his house on 30th Place N.W. was chock full of memorabilia.

floor of the master bedroom's balcony. "He was a strange man," Spitzer says. "He really loved gardening—we kept a few of his rose bushes. But then there was this Astroturf."

They took off the famous bulletproof windows. Spitzer says the bulletproofing on the windows covered only the bottom half, which is waist-high on her: "I know he was short, but. . ."

Dead Drops
Cabin John Regional Park
10600 Westlake Drive, Bethesda

One of the more ingenious drop sites on record was one an East Berlin courier invented. He always made copies of the documents he delivered to the Soviets—just in case. These papers he hid in two 25-liter plastic water jugs which he buried in a "grave" in a remote corner of an East Berlin cemetery.

For other documents—especially the green kind with numbers—the loose brick in the wall, the hollowed-out log or the tree stump is preferred. For years, a favorite Soviet dead drop was a very large oak tree at a busy intersection in Northwest Washington. Bad trade-craft to use a drop site more than once.

Bethesda's Cabin John Park is best known for its playground, kiddie train and ice skating rink. But in 1982, Glenn Michael Souther took one of his girlfriends there to help him look for $4,000 concealed in logs or stumps. Souther was a sexually fixated Navy photographer with a bizarre sense of humor who passed top secret spy-satellite photos and nuclear war plans on to the Soviets.

Essentially, he was in the park to pick up his paycheck. His girlfriend told the FBI that at various times she also saw him take down coded messages from a shortwave radio, decipher messages using a code book or one-time pad, put colored tape on a phone booth and use microfilm hidden in a pen. He also engaged in countersurveillance techniques to throw off possible pursuers—"drycleaning" himself by driving at 80 miles an hour then slowing down to 20. She wasn't sure he was spying, though.

In 1986, just when the FBI was about to go after him, Souther disappeared. Friends and family had all but given him up as lost when newspapers reported that he had shown up in Moscow seeking asylum. Then, in 1989, though he had been made an officer in the KGB, he killed himself.

Club Jed
Congressional Country Club
8500 River Road, Potomac

Congressional Country Club's golf course sprawls languidly on the doorstep of Potomac hunt country. The main clubhouse, modeled after a Spanish villa—white stucco with a red tile roof and wrought-iron balconies—has aged so agreeably that one can almost imagine it in the hills above Marbella on the Costa del Sol.

Like so many seasoned beauties, the country club has a past. During World War II, it was known as Area F—an OSS training area for operational groups (OGs). The OGs were teams of highly trained, multi-lingual soldiers, accomplished parachutists to be dropped behind the lines to harass the enemy.

The Spanish villa clubhouse served as Area F headquarters. Wood-and-canvas tents sprouted up around it for the trainees. The golf course was transformed into obstacle courses, patrolling courses, firing ranges and demolition ranges.

Among the OGs were the famous Jedburghs: three-man teams consisting of two officers and one radio operator. Having prepared no cover stories, they were to give only name, rank and serial number if captured in enemy territory. Jedburgh teams helped the local resistance in sabotaging enemy communications, destroying fuel and ammo dumps and collecting intelligence. As the OSS was a breeding ground for the next generation of intelligence, it is not surprising that at least two future CIA directors were involved in Jedburgh operations. As a "Jed," William Colby parachuted behind enemy lines in France after D-Day; William Casey ran the Jedburgh teams toward the end of the war.

By that time, recruiting and training at the country club had been replaced by rest and relaxation. It became a Reallocation Center where returning OSS agents were debriefed and given psychological tests.

Having reverted completely to private R and R, Congressional

Country Club now has a long waiting list. The wait is at least 12 years, and membership is not free.

The Game of Soviet Pursuit
Various drop sites in Potomac

Former Navy warrant officer John A. Walker, Jr., provided the Soviets with the keys to U.S. naval communications for more than 20 years ("If I had access to a secret, color it gone"). He recruited his brother and even his own son. Arrested in the early morning hours of May 20, 1985, he is serving a life sentence in prison. His "last ride" took him from Norfolk, Virginia, to drop sites in Montgomery County, Maryland.

If Walker's ride were a game, it would be called "Soviet Pursuit—Drop Site!" It would be created by "Walker Brothers," of course. Players could match wits with the FBI while exchanging secret documents with Soviet agents for cash. On computer, it would be another "Adventure" game.

Walker was under constant surveillance at the time it all went down. Twenty cars full of FBI agents followed his van from Norfolk on Saturday, May 18. Just in case the suspect was on the alert, they kept passing him in their cars, then slowing down and changing disguises, then passing him again.

Driving on the Beltway, Walker passed into Maryland. To blend in, many of the agents stopped and changed their license plates accordingly. Then Walker did a strange thing. He drove around Potomac, slowing down at certain intersections and looking hard at certain utility poles. He was reviewing his drop sites, and the FBI duly noted them. Late in the afternoon, the agents lost him. About 50 agents regrouped behind the Safeway at Potomac Center at Falls and River Roads. They later learned that their quarry had gone to the Ramada Hotel in Rockville on Route 28 and had checked in under the name of Joe Johnson.

The agents set up "picket surveillance" at every key intersection. It wasn't long before they picked up the scent again. At 7:48 P.M., Walker was spotted driving up River Road near Potomac Center.

Walker was following a set of instructions from his Soviet handlers that described an intricate dance that would take four hours to complete. The Soviet KGB and GRU officers loved Potomac. For one thing, Soviet diplomats were not allowed to go more than 25 miles from the White House without permission. And Potomac has so many nice trees and, especially in the northern reaches, stretches of quiet road. Perfect for drop sites.

Walker hit a number of drop sites that night. First, he drove around looking for a 7-Up can. His handler instructed: "To signal that I am ready to exchange, I'll drop my initial can of the usual kind at a utility pole on Watts Branch Drive near its intersection with Circle Drive and Ridge Drive."

To clarify matters, the handler enclosed photographs of each drop site from different angles and a map.

At 8:30, Walker left a 7-Up can at the base of a utility pole on Quince Orchard Road at Dufief Mill Road, which signaled to the Soviets that he was ready to make the exchange. A confused FBI agent picked up the can. Because the Soviets didn't find the can when they looked for it, as far as they knew, Walker wasn't playing for some reason.

Walker didn't know he was out of the game, however, and left his secret documents behind a utility pole next to a large tree on Partnership Road at Whites Ferry Road. On the surface, his drop appeared to be a brown paper bag filled with empty Coke bottles and cereal boxes. But the "trash" was clean. Underneath was a plastic bag sealed with tape and holding 129 classified documents.

Walker drove to Old Bucklodge Lane at White Ground Road to retrieve his cash payment, which was to be left behind two forked trees. He had no way of knowing that the FBI, not the Soviets, had scooped up his documents. Payment would not be forthcoming.

At midnight, Walker gave up looking for it and went back to the Ramada Hotel, to his room on the seventh floor. At 3:30 A.M., an FBI agent posing as a hotel clerk phoned his room to tell him that someone had broken into his van in the parking lot. Walker decided the call was legitimate. But when he got up and walked into the hallway, he heard the dreaded words: "FBI! Freeze!"

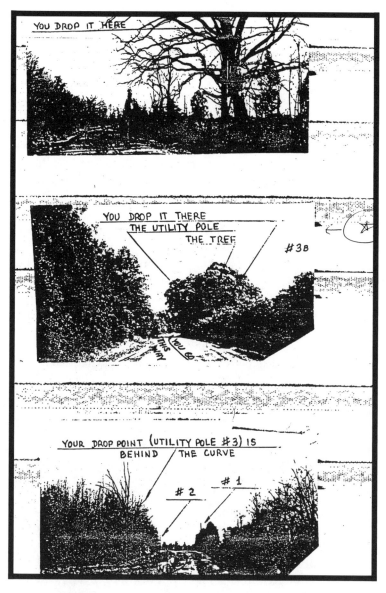

KGB drop-site instructions to spy John A. Walker, Jr.

Thee Name It, We Have It
Sandy Spring Store
905 Olney-Sandy Spring Road, Olney

The Sandy Spring Store has gone through a lot of physical changes since it was built in 1819. But the general store is still running, and some old sections of the building remain. "The cellar is one year older than God," says Nancy Barton, one of the current owners. "We do have a hardwood floor, which of course has been here donkeys' ages. And there are several antique scales and meat racks I can show you in the back."

Once, while digging in the yard, Barton found a Union belt buckle and a cartridge case. "Most of the people that were on my property were Union," she says. During the Civil War, the store served the local Quaker community, selling such goods as oranges, lemons, kerosene, plows and hoopskirts.

The store played a role in the Battle of Rickett's Run, a small skirmish that ended in the death of a Confederate agent. Walter "Wat" Bowie, a native of Prince George's County who had a long handlebar moustache, was like many of his neighbors a Southern sympathizer. Before joining Mosby's Rangers, he had served as scout and courier, running the Union picket lines in the early years of the war, crossing and recrossing the Potomac by ferry, gathering messages, medical supplies and intelligence for Richmond. Now a captain under Mosby's command, the former agent had just been to Annapolis in an aborted plan to kidnap the governor of Maryland.

After the plan fell through, on the night of October 6, 1864, on his way past the Sandy Spring Store, Bowie was attracted to the merchandise. He even had a list. His men threatened to hang the store's clerk if he didn't let them in. The clerk obliged and later recalled that the Rebs took "a little of everything and a goodeal of somethings," including kid gloves, cravats, sashes and slippers. They also relieved him of his boots. They helped themselves to food and went off, resting at Rickett's Run, a stream a few miles north of Rockville.

Meanwhile, the offended clerk back at Sandy Spring helped raise

Confederate spy "Wat" Bowie got greedy at the Sandy Spring Store and died for it.

The death of the Rebel spy "Wat" Bowie, as illustrated in special provost marshal Lafayette C. Baker's autobiography.

a posse. The trail of stolen hats and cravats was easy to follow. The posse—a third of which was made up of otherwise peaceable Quakers—found the marauders asleep and ambushed them. As the clerk recalled, just as Bowie was passing by, "Old Ent who was concealed behind a pine bush let him have a whole load of buckshot in the face and upper part of the head which knocked him sky high."

Dog Days at the FBI
Aspen Hill Memorial Park
13630 Georgia Avenue, Wheaton

The grieving family slowly walks behind a casket so small that it needs only one man to carry it. The freshly cut grass smells sweet and clean. A dog barks from a neighboring yard. If any words are said over the dear departed, they are nothing planned. There is no service.

Here in Aspen Hill Memorial Park, the epitaphs say it all: "Dickie Dave, aged 15 years. Beloved, infinitely sweet little loved one, come back to me." "Nala—He's a good boy." "To Bingo, Puffy, Ginger, Blackie, Tubby, Pee Wee, Lucky and Stinkie," from "George and Mother." Scattered among dozens of child-sized statues of Saint Francis of Assisi are the final resting places of Topsy, Micky, Mousie, Tony Darling, Hy-Jinks and Trouble, not to mention Trimmy and Twummy, Tinsel and Scruffy Muffin. There are more placid plastic rabbits and spinning whirligigs here than at any roadside stand. Instead of a plastic flower arrangement, a mourning master has marked the spot with two yellow tennis balls, now fading, unbitten, in their metal holders.

Let us linger now at the grave of Spee De Bozo, a worthy wight, perhaps fleet of paw and slow of brain, perhaps of French extraction. His epitaph: "Our Best Friend." The dog was once best friend to J. Edgar Hoover (nickname: Speedy), the late formidable director of the FBI. (He himself is buried in Congressional Cemetery.) At the time of the dog's death, Hoover's nemesis John Dillinger was still

Pamela Kessler

A headstone at the Aspen Hill Memorial Park, where J. Edgar Hoover's dogs are buried, bears a striking resemblance to the late director.

at large on a killing spree, and gang member Baby Face Nelson had just shot an FBI agent.

Rumor has it that at least seven Hoover dogs are buried here, though the cemetery can verify only four. During his 50-year reign, it would conceivably have been very useful for the unsavory elements to know that the hard man who inspired so much fear had a soft spot.

Sigint City
National Security Agency
at Fort Meade, off the Baltimore-Washington Parkway on Route 32

N SA intercepts communications worldwide, from intercept stations everywhere. It has more entrance requirements than the most exclusive country club.

Halfway between Washington and Baltimore, NSA headquarters is one of those spy sites most people have less than brush-contact with—a fenced-in cluster of massive office buildings, featureless except for the paraphernalia on the roof—antennas, microwave dishes and giant golfballs. The icy aquamarine window surfaces mean NSA can see out, but you can't see in.

Some call this sprawling complex "Sigint City"—after signal intelligence, its specialty. It has its own barber, banking facilities, travel agency, medical center, bus service, police force, college (the National Cryptologic School) and TV station. This town is big enough for both protecting classified U.S. communications and intercepting foreign ones.

Inside, NSA processes the harvest of electronic emissions it has caught in its net throughout the world. Sometimes the cryptologists' work requires converting signals hidden within the radio spectrum— for instance, a message secretly burst on an oldies' radio station during an innocent airing of "I Heard it Through the Grapevine." The name of the current game is "spread spectrum," which operates on a variety of frequencies; a signal sent this way is nearly hopelessly lost to anyone not holding the keys to its retrieval. Needless to say, with this sort of challenge, the supercomputers at crypto central are the biggest and best in the world.

Unfortunately, a fishing net leaks both ways. In 1959, two "cryppies," Bernon F. Mitchell and William H. Martin, became disenchanted with NSA. They broke silence (and the law) when they blew the whistle to Congressman Wayne Hays (D-Ohio) about flights over Russia to ferret out radar responses. Such deliberate violation of airspace was playing with fire, they thought—nuclear holocaust. When the two men got no response from Congress, they took a long vacation in July 1960 and ended up in Moscow. Though the HUAC damage report implied that their primary reason for defecting was homosexuality, it seems clear that Mitchell and Martin were true ideological defectors. They left a farewell note saying that the U.S. government was "as unscrupulous as it has accused the Soviet Government of being." Within a few years, both men became disillusioned again, this time with the Soviet Union. But they were stuck.

More recently, financial problems inspired an NSA mole, Ronald W. Pelton. Pelton was a major disaster for the agency. In the seventies, he worked for NSA as a communications specialist. Codenamed MR. LONG, he was a walk-in to the Soviet embassy in January 1980. He gave away a number of top-secret operations—revealing Project Ivy Bells, which was an NSA tap on a Soviet undersea cable that carried military communications, and identifying for the Soviets which transmissions NSA wanted to intercept. Five years later, during his short-lived defection, KGB Colonel Vitaly Yurchenko fingered Mr. Long. The FBI tracked him down and cornered him in a game of good-cop bad-cop in Room 409 at the Annapolis Hilton. Convicted of espionage in 1986, Pelton got life.

The Fifth Column
Surratt House and Tavern
9110 Brandywine Road, Clinton

Almost every postmaster in Southern Maryland was a Confederate sympathizer, said special provost marshal Lafayette C. Baker, in his reminiscences about his role in the Civil War. "Rebel emissaries were constantly conveying information from Washington to the post-offices along the Potomac, from which it was transmitted to Fredericksburg by blockade-runners and spies, and thence telegraphed to Richmond," Baker wrote, referring to one of several routes.

As a Southern Maryland postmaster, John Harrison Surratt was no exception. His sympathies were known. His post office, tavern, polling place, farm and home—"Surratt's Villa"—stood at a popular crossroads in Surrattsville (now Clinton). When he died suddenly in 1862, his wife, Mary Surratt, whose heart was also with the Rebels, took over the tavern operation. Their son John Jr. became a courier for the Confederacy. And, while Union officers would stop there for food and drink, the Surratt Tavern continued as a safehouse for the Confederate underground network.

The tavern still stands, open for tours, a red-shingled house across from an Exxon station, around the corner from a shopping center, near a candy-striped water tower. Inside, the air is thick with the pleasant farmhouse smell of yellowing linens and mellowing floors. There are a few belongings here that had been Mary Surratt's: in the parlor, an Empire table and a lady's desk with fruitwood inlay and gilding in the leg; in the museum, her 18th-century watch, a family heirloom even back when she owned it. Though she had to move to her H Street boarding house in 1864 when she could no longer keep up the tavern, she was not poor.

There is much talk here about John Wilkes Booth's having stopped at the tavern after the Lincoln assassination, to pick up a package from the tenant, John Lloyd, which Lloyd had gotten to-

MARY SURRATT
1823-1865

Mary Surratt ran a Confederate safehouse in southern Maryland, and the Lincoln conspirators met at her boarding house in D.C. For her suspected role in the assassination, she was the first woman ever executed by the U.S. government.

Surratt's Tavern was a safehouse and mail drop for the Confederacy's Secret Line through Maryland.

gether as per Mary Surratt's instructions. But the tavern's history lasted longer than one fateful night. It was part of the underground that included the "doctor's line" out of Washington—men who had reason to travel about, with ciphers and missives in their medicine cases. Surratt's was a safehouse and mail drop on the Secret Line through Maryland, by which agents and scouts could forward letters, papers, messages and small packages. At first, "Little Johnny" Surratt was a dispatch carrier along this line. Later, his job territory expanded. He carried dispatches from Richmond to Confederate agents in Canada.

That explains why he was out of town those fateful days in April 1865. John Surratt had been part of the original Booth plan to kidnap Lincoln, and he had brought Booth and some of his friends to his mother's boarding house. Some say he was in Elmira, New York, to check out a prison camp; others more romantic say he was smuggling out the last of the Confederate gold. Whatever he was up to, as soon as he heard reports of Lincoln's death, he hightailed it into Canada and then Europe, staying there during his mother's imprisonment and execution. When he returned to Washington two years later to be brought up on similar charges, he was acquitted, public outrage by that time having dropped from its rabid, post-assassination level.

The Andersonville of the North
Point Lookout State Park
Route 5, St. Marys County (301) 872-5688

Point Lookout couldn't be any better placed strategically. It is a tip of land washed by the Potomac River on the west and the Chesapeake Bay on the east. Ships heading from the ocean north toward Washington have to pass the point. And so at dawn on August 17, 1814, when Thomas Swann, a Washington lawyer, took up watch, he was able to spot the British fleet bearing steadily up the bay. He sent a courier to ride the 70 miles to warn the capital. But such a journeyman's job of surveillance couldn't stop the British. They landed at Bladensburg, marched unopposed to Washington and burned it.

During the Civil War, Point Lookout served another purpose: It was the site of Camp Hoffman, a prisoner-of-war camp that has been called the Andersonville of the North. As in the notorious Confederate POW camp in Georgia, conditions were deplorable. Camp Hoffman was the only Union POW camp that housed its prisoners in tents. Blankets and rations were scarce, and water had to be shipped in daily from Washington.

Confederate soldiers started arriving after the Battle of Gettysburg, but the first prisoners, in early 1863, were locals. They were representatives of Southern Maryland's extensive fifth column of Southern sympathizers, blockade runners and couriers.

By June 1864, more than 20,000 Confederates were incarcerated there, including one woman soldier, a private, discovered during the usual strip search at the wharf. Of course there was always the hope that one would find a battle plan stuffed in a soldier's pocket. And it is an ancient practice to interrogate prisoners of war in hopes of eliciting military intelligence. Human intelligence was even more important in those days when tradecraft aids were limited to observation balloons and the newly invented telegraph.

Today there is a museum on the point, with an exhibit of weapons, uniforms and crafts the prisoners made and used for barter: an intricate fan, oyster shell tie-pins, miniature rocking chairs made from scrap. One of Point Lookout's three forts still stands, Fort Lincoln, built in 1864 by Confederate soldiers supervised by Union guards. Part of the earthworks that encompassed the prison camp has been reconstructed, and you can still see the road that led up to it from the wharf.

The One Who Cracked
Overlook Two, northbound on the George Washington Memorial Parkway

Two men sat in a car at the second overlook on the G.W. Parkway and watched the lights of Northwest Washington across the river. It was seven o'clock at night, on Friday, January 12, 1973. Through an intermediary, James McCord, Jr., a defendant in the Watergate burglary, had agreed to meet here with John Caulfield, a White House staff member. The intermediary, Tony Ulasewicz, had relayed this message to McCord from John Dean, the President's counsel: Plead guilty.

As the late rush-hour cars hissed behind them, McCord said that no offer of jobs when he got out of jail and no promise to take care of his family impressed him. He wanted his freedom. If he went down, anyone else involved would go with him. He asked Caulfield to tell him who had made the offer of clemency. Caulfield assured him it came "from the highest level of the White House."

Two days later, on Sunday afternoon, they met again at the same place. This time, Caulfield and McCord got out of their cars and walked from the overlook down the steep path toward the Potomac River. To the north they could see Chain Bridge; to the south, Fletcher's Boat House. It was possible to feel remote from Washington here.

The White House officials were complaining, said Caulfield, that McCord was the only Watergate burglary defendant refusing to co-operate. The message was clear: He should take executive clemency and go to prison quietly, and there would be financial aid (some of the "hush money" that would be paid the original defendants).

Two months later, nine months after the break-in at Democratic National Committee headquarters, McCord sang to the Senate Watergate Committee and grand juries. The former CIA employee was the first of the conspirators to implicate high officials in the White

House in the Watergate case. Apparently because of his cooperation with government prosecutors, his sentence was lightened to one to five years.

In the Line of Duty
Arlington National Cemetery
Off the George Washington Memorial Parkway at Memorial Bridge

At Arlington Cemetery, a man comes into the visitor's center and asks the clerk behind the counter, "Could you tell me what you have to do to be buried here?"

"Besides the obvious?" the clerk replies.

Generally, a long stint in the military is a requirement. It also helps to be a hero. For instance, Richard Welch, a CIA officer who died in the line of duty, was never in the military. But through presidential order this small fact was overlooked so he could be buried here. Occasionally, the system breaks down. Sergeant Jack E. Dunlap, though he had been awarded the Purple Heart and Bronze Star for bravery in Korea, was anything but an American hero. What these two men have in common, besides a piece of hallowed ground, is that they were both spies—albeit for opposing sides.

A rustling among the leaves, the leaves scattering across the headstones in the chill wind. The visitor who tramps along Arlington Cemetery's 612 acres will find, among the more than 219,000 people buried here, spies like these, as well as Robert Ames and Francis Gary Powers.

To the disappointment of some at the CIA, Powers did not push the destruct button on his U-2 surveillance plane before bailing out over the Soviet Union in 1960. Once captured, he did not stick himself with the suicide pin charged with shellfish toxin and concealed in a silver dollar. Nevertheless, five years later, safely home, he was awarded the Intelligence Star, one of the CIA's highest honors. He had served two years of his jail sentence in Russia when he

RICHARD S
WELCH
CENTRAL
INTELLIGENCE
AGENCY
UNITED STATES
OF
AMERICA
DECEMBER 14 1929
DECEMBER 23 1975

Pamela Kessler

*Buried at Arlington National Cemetery, former CIA station chief
Richard S. Welch was honored with a headstone naming his employer.*

was traded for KGB agent Rudolph Abel. When Powers died, it was in 1977, while working as a traffic reporter for a Los Angeles radio station. He was killed in a Cessna crash.

Richard Welch was chief of station in Athens—the head of CIA operations in Greece—when his cover as first secretary of the embassy was blown. His name had first appeared in 1967 in an East German publication, *Who's Who in the CIA*. Then in 1975, *CounterSpy*, an anti-CIA newsletter, reminded everyone who he was. In that issue, a disaffected former CIA officer, Philip Agee, wrote, "The most effective and important systematic efforts to combat the CIA that can be taken right now are, I think, the identification, exposure and neutralization of its people working abroad." On November 25, *Athens News* picked up the story, publishing Welch's name and home address. Less than a month later, he was shot dead on his doorstep. His headstone bears an unusual epitaph: Central Intelligence Agency.

Like Welch, Robert Ames has the words Central Intelligence Agency on his headstone. As national intelligence officer for the Mideast, he was visiting Beirut when a suicide truck-bomb drove into the American embassy in Lebanon on April 18, 1983. Among the 16 other Americans killed were CIA officers whose names were never publicly revealed. But it is said that they too are buried in Arlington Cemetery.

Jack Dunlap's story begins at the end. A month after his burial in Arlington on July 25, 1963, his widow reported that she had found classified papers among his belongings. Death cancels everything but truth. The Army sergeant had worked five years for NSA—much of the time, it turned out, feeding secrets to the Soviets.

Two major security foul-ups helped him in this pursuit. First, NSA typically didn't run its own clearance checks but took the Army's word on the personnel they assigned to Fort Meade; and second, even low-level personnel such as Dunlap, who worked variously as chauffeur and messenger, had access to highly classified material.

Dunlap liked the life—his newly acquired mistress and his sky-blue Jaguar, his Cadillac convertible, his yellow Caddy sedan, his championship speedboat. Although he parked daily in the Fort Meade parking lot, no one seemed to wonder how a $100-a-week messenger could afford to drive a Jag. No one noticed the documents tucked under his shirt when he left the building either. Finally, he did excite some interest when, worried he'd be sent overseas when his tour of duty was over, he applied to leave the Army, hoping to keep his job at NSA as a civilian. Now at last he was subjected to polygraph tests, which he failed. Then, when investigators learned he was living beyond his means, the Army transferred him to another Fort Meade job with no access to secrets.

Despondent and justifiably paranoid, one night Dunlap drove to a deserted road on Markey's Creek, not far from NSA. He had bought a bottle of good Scotch and borrowed a radiator hose from the motor pool. Attaching the hose to his car's tailpipe, he looped it in through the front window on the passenger's side and turned on the motor. Fishermen found him dead the next morning.

He was buried at Arlington with full military honors.

The Color PURPLE
Arlington Hall
South George Mason Drive and U.S. 50, Arlington

Barbed wire fencing marks the boundaries of Arlington Hall along Route 50. Once a girls' school, it is chiefly remembered as the home of the Signal Intelligence Service (SIS), which moved here in 1942. After the war it became the Army Security Agency (ASA). Along with the crypto departments of the Navy and Air Force, the ASA was put under the umbrella organization, the Armed Forces Security Agency. In 1952, the AFSA turned into NSA. Acronym begets acronym.

From the roads around this small government reservation, the only significant structure visible is the administration building. Temporary buildings that once surrounded it are gone, along with their thousand or so single-room air-conditioners. The original head of the SIS, William Friedman, had his office in the administration building. He was a dapper man with bowtie and moustache, given to wearing two-toned shoes.

During the war, Arlington Hall was the American version of Bletchley Park, an estate in England that housed replicas of the

German ENIGMA cipher machines. The product of the British efforts was dubbed ULTRA. At Arlington Hall, with replicas of the Japanese PURPLE machines, American cryptologists produced MAGIC. It was here that the SIS broke the main cryptosystems used by the Japanese army. Japanese military attachés unwittingly communicated useful information about the Nazis—which was a bonus for those who were reading their mail.

The SIS shared the processing of Purple traffic with the Naval Security Group (NSG). While both worked on diplomatic traffic, each had its own targets: the Japanese and German Army for the SIS; the Japanese and German Navy for the NSG.

The Army's cryptologic section continued to work out of Arlington Hall until 1990. Now the State Department is slated to use it as a training area, so the signs still apply: "U.S. Government Property, No Trespassing." From the parking lot behind the shopping center at South Glebe Road and U.S. 50, one can see strange, fenced-in pods in the fenced-in woods. They have their own level

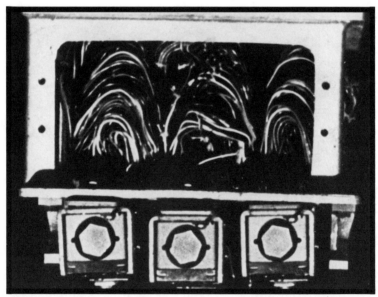

National Archives

Although it looked like avant-garde sculpture, the American copy of the Japanese PURPLE machine was used at Arlington Hall to decipher Japanese military codes.

of security, their own crop of warning signs: "No construction personnel allowed in area—$500 fine."

Was it just coincidence that a favorite haunt of defector Vitaly Yurchenko was a pizza joint in this shopping center, back in the late seventies when he was chief of security at the Soviet Embassy? So close to the Army Security Agency? Haltehs is a family-run place, with an innocent air imparted by perpetual TV and a constant stream of take-out customers. However, Yurchenko always stayed to eat, and always the same thing. Something must have been lacking in his American diet to make him order anchovy pizza.

Trolling
Wildwood Towers
1075 South Jefferson Street, Arlington

During the Cold War, FBI counterintelligence squads in Washington ran a cat-and-mouse game with Soviet intelligence officers using diplomatic cover. Both sides took turns at playing mouse.

The Soviets worked out a simple plan for gathering information. Called trolling, it depended on the feeding-and-drinking frenzy after work. Draw a circle around any office building, and fan out, and you'll find the employees' hangouts. The Soviets applied this principle to Northern Virginia, where the proximity of the Pentagon promises a high concentration of military personnel. The Soviets would stalk the bars and restaurants, looking for unhappy people getting smashed, and then spring: "Are you a regular? Where do you work? You look like you've got something on your mind. . . ." It never hurt to play when once in a blue moon you could win the lottery.

Because of the military installations, Soviet intelligence officers also found it convenient to reside in Northern Virginia. GRU officer Vladimir Ismaylov was no exception. It was ironic that his modest, if not bleak Arlington apartment building, with aluminum balconies holding bicycles and dead plants, was reminiscent of architecture in Moscow.

Ismaylov would see home again sooner than he thought. One night in an Arlington bar in 1985, he tried to recruit a high-ranking Air Force officer. The man played along but reported the contact to the Air Force. Whereas each military service has its own investigative branch to ferret out spies within, counterintelligence is the FBI's bailiwick, and the case went to them. As everyone who works with the FBI apparently must have a codename, they dubbed the Air Force officer YOGI. Yogi agreed to become a double agent.

The cat thus became the mouse. Yogi met with Ismaylov at various locations in Northern Virginia, the Belle View Shopping Center in Alexandria being one favorite rendezvous point. And there were various local drop sites where Yogi would bury the documents Ismaylov was buying. Declassified for the purpose of baiting the Soviet, the documents were the real thing.

In June 1986, Ismaylov dug up his last batch. On Riverview Road in Fort Washington, Maryland, across the Wilson Bridge from

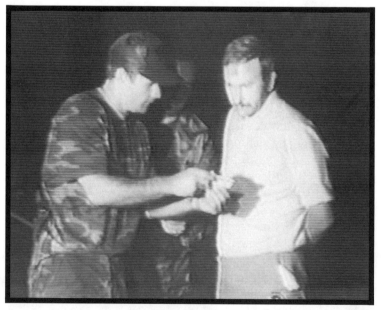

Federal Bureau of Investigation

Caught in the act of digging up fake classified documents, GRU officer Vladimir M. Ismaylov is arrested in Fort Washington, Maryland.

Alexandria, the FBI caught him just as he crouched at the base of a certain PEPCO utility pole and started to dig. Ismaylov was declared *persona non grata* and returned to the Soviet Union.

The First Spymaster
Mount Vernon
George Washington Parkway, Alexandria

At Mount Vernon, the docents who guide visitors through the rooms of the main house talk about George Washington as wealthy planter, soldier, statesman, first president and father of his country. But they leave out the fact that he was also this country's first spymaster.

Pamela Kessler

An arcaded breezeway at Mount Vernon, the plantation of the first American spymaster.

I intreat you to exert your best endeavors to obtain every useful intelligence you possibly can of the Enemy's motions by Sea and Land, in doing this Money may be required, and do not spare it. Communicate everything of Importance to me with dispatch. . .

—George Washington to
Brigadier-General Hugh Mercer, 1776

Washington didn't actually run spies out of his plantation. He was away for the war, except for September 9 through 12, 1781, on his way down to Yorktown and British surrender, and on his return, November 13 through 20. So there is little at Mount Vernon to link him to his pioneering role in American military intelligence— save a couple of spyglasses for observing the enemy unobserved, which he purchased during the war.

One reason we don't typically think of Washington as spymaster is the 200-year-old habit of soft-pedaling American espionage during the Revolution. The leaders wanted it to appear that, unlike the British, we were above such shenanigans. The tale wasn't told until 1821, when James Fenimore Cooper's book *The Spy* came out. In addition, the cherry-tree school of thought ("I cannot tell a lie," said George) prevents some of us from seeing the first president as capable of guile, even on behalf of his country.

But run spies he did. With Major Benjamin Tallmadge's spy network, the Culper Ring, reporting directly to him on any "uncommon movements" in New York and Long Island, Washington was able to maneuver around the enemy. Early in the war, before congressional appropriations, he had paid for intelligence gathering himself. His personal tradecraft ran to disappearing ink, then known as "secret writing" and "sympathetic stain." He understood the value of intercepted letters, accounts from POWs and deserters, and reports in newspapers, which he would exchange with his generals in other cities. He believed that the best agents were recruited from among one's friends.

He was always on the lookout for "false information" but wasn't above putting out his own: slipping forged documents into intercepted British pouches before sending them on their way, and allowing his couriers to be captured with bogus messages. False information called for consistency: When one is deceiving the enemy with "false opinions" of superior troop numbers, he noted, any calls for additional enlistments should be done quietly. But it worked both ways: the general himself was sometimes burned by false information and double agents.

Washington had a subtle deviousness of mind. His deception schemes included leaving a noisy group behind for the night to keep the campfires burning while the rest of the army marched on. Once, when one of his generals unwittingly captured one of Washington's own spies, Washington counseled his adjutant general who was handling intelligence to engineer the spy's escape. As a "fugitive from the persecution and danger," he would return to the enemy flush with "a handsome present in money," not to mention redoubled credibility. As Washington wrote on April 7, 1777:

> Great care must be taken, so to conduct the scheme, as to make the escape appear natural and real; there must be neither too much facility, nor too much refinement, and doing too little, or over acting the part, would, alike beget a suspicion of the true state of the case.

Letters and circulars to his officers offer a basic, common-sense guide to intelligence. His letters were shopping lists for necessary information—the gathering of troops, the collecting of horses and the building of boats—and he knew how to use it. He was his own intelligence analyst. Like all chiefs, he wanted his information sooner rather than later: "The good effect of Intelligence may be lost if it is not speedily transmitted," he wrote. A true believer in the Eyes-Only concept, Washington preferred to receive his intelligence in writing.

Despite his sagacity in matters of spying, Washington did have the occasional blind spot. Codenames or pseudonyms, for example. As he wrote to one of his intelligence officers: "It runs in my head that I was to corrispond with you by a fictitious name, if so I have forgotten the name and must be reminded of it again."

At Sea at a Covert Interrogation Center
Fort Hunt
George Washington Parkway, Alexandria

On the surface it would seem
that Fort Hunt's broad, grassy parkland has known nothing more
heated than a softball game. In times of conflict, the fort never fired
so much as a rifle. But beyond the picnic pavilion, the pine grove
and ball fields, a row of abandoned gun emplacements hints at history. During the Spanish-American War, Fort Hunt was a crossfire-
companion to Fort Washington across the river. Earlier in this century, it functioned as a training camp for black officers and a Civilian
Conservation Corps camp.

During World War II, it was a top-secret interrogation center
for newly captured German prisoners, usually U-boat personnel. A

Pamela Kessler

Graceful rows of trees at Fort Hunt belie its history as an illegal
interrogation center for German U-boat personnel during World War II.

124

large electrical fence surrounded two prison complexes with a capacity of 110. During its three years of operation, 3,451 prisoners passed through the camp. The sailors stayed no longer than three weeks, a sort of debriefing period before the Red Cross would be notified and the men sent to a regular POW camp. The delay, and the camp itself, were illegal but considered small infractions when weighed against the number of ships the U.S. was losing to U-boats off the East Coast.

Inexperienced at interrogation, the Americans learned more about the German submarine service through eavesdropping on the prison cells, which were outfitted with microphones. According to Sandra Weber, a National Park Service historian, some of the prisoners suspected they were being overheard. They whiled away the hours by singing, imitating animal noises and telling obscene stories for the benefit of their listeners.

As records of Fort Hunt operations have only recently been declassified, it remains to be seen whether the interrogation center was a worthwhile intelligence operation that helped turn the tide against the U-boats.

The Search for Sasha
Gallery Orlov
1307 King Street, Alexandria

Sasha existed. The mole that Golytsin predicted would be found in the CIA was real.

But Sasha was no longer working for the CIA. The agency had terminated him in 1961. And he was never an employee—just on contract. The man who fit the profile was Igor Orlov, a Russian who began working for the CIA in Germany in 1949. After instructing Orlov to come to the United States, the agency severed ties with him. He was never the big cheese that Golytsin kept describing to his mentor, counterintelligence chief James Angleton. (See page 132.)

Several defectors fingered Orlov, and the FBI tried without success to make a case against him. In 1963, the bureau searched Orlov's home and art gallery, Gallery Orlov in Alexandria. They found nothing incriminating.

It's hard enough to make an espionage case that will hold up in court when a spy is still engaged in intelligence activities. It's virtually impossible when he is no longer active. So there was nothing to be done.

Orlov briefly sought refuge in the Soviet embassy, telling his wife, Eleonore, he had gone there only to obtain information about his Russian relatives. If he should die, he told her, he wanted her to take his ashes to the embassy, which he hoped would send them back to the Soviet Union. When Orlov died in 1982, the FBI's investigation was closed.

Vitaly Yurchenko, during his brief defection of 1985, fingered Orlov again.

Life goes on at the little gallery on King Street, which specializes in Old World scenic prints. Eleonore Orlov has been interviewed so often about her late husband that her gallery is something of a hangout for espionage writers.

Confederate Heroine?
The Ford Building
3977 Chain Bridge Road, Fairfax

The short but interesting life of Antonia Ford began in a dormered red brick house across from Fairfax courthouse, at 3977 Chain Bridge Road. The Daughters of the Confederacy have remembered their "Confederate Heroine" with a plaque by the entrance. And she would feel right at home next door at the Black-Eyed Pea with its "home cookin'"—corn bread, okra, red beans and rice, and chicken' n' dumplings. The waiters can spot a Yankee here; it's whoever asks them to hold the ice cream, a scoop being standard Dixie on the pie or cobbler.

Pamela Kessler

The Ford Building in downtown Fairfax was the home of sometime
Confederate spy and socialite Antonia Ford.

The Ford home, now attorneys' offices, was visited by troops from both sides during the Civil War. When sweet-faced Antonia Ford entertained the Union officers garrisoned at Fairfax Station, she reportedly passed on the information she gleaned—location of officers' quarters, picket points, troop strength—to Jeb Stuart and to John Mosby, whose raiders were gradually transforming Northern Virginia into "Mosby's Confederacy."

When special provost marshal Lafayette Baker sent a female undercover agent to visit her and play Secessionist, the agent learned of Antonia Ford's "commission." This was a letter from Jeb Stuart naming her his honorary aide-de-camp: "She will be obeyed, respected and admired by all the lovers of a noble nature," he had written. More playfully affectionate than the typical military commission, it casts some doubt on the seriousness of her role.

But at the time, it was incriminating enough. She was arrested twice and put in the Old Capitol Prison. The first time she was released she was sent south. The irrepressible Antonia Ford returned. The second time she was released, she signed a loyalty oath. Witness to her signing was a Union major, Joseph C. Willard, well acquainted with her—in love, in fact. He was the founder, with his brother Henry, of the Willard Hotel on Pennsylvania Avenue. Apparently, Joseph and Antonia had mutually agreed to renounce all other loyalties: He resigned from the army, divorced his wife and, in 1864, married her. Antonia Ford bore three sons and, having married well, was able to become, once again, the gracious hostess. She died seven years later at the age of 33. It was said that her imprisonment had ruined her health.

The Perfect Cover
National Historical Intelligence Museum
(703)578-6880

The National Historical Intelligence Museum is as elusive as its subject, the spy. It has no location. In May 1991, it opened briefly in a meeting room at the Reserve

Officers Association in the District then passed again from existence at summer's end. Rest assured it will reopen, if only temporarily—date and place unknown. The museum awaits funding and hopes for a permanent home and its own collection some day. In the recent exhibit, artifacts on loan—such as a one-time pad, a suitcase radio-direction finder and an easily concealed mini-camera—took a back seat to the message: Espionage was, is, and ever shall be part of government operations. For emphasis, the exhibit cites, in the way of all true believers, the Bible: "And Moses sent them to spy out the land of Canaan, and said unto them. . .'see the land, what it is; and the people that dwelleth therein, whether they be strong or weak, few or many. . .'" (Numbers 13:17–18).

Jeb Stuart's Secret Muse
Laura Ratcliffe Hanna's gravesite
The Worldgate Centre, Herndon

Most drivers on busy Centreville Road don't notice the small family cemetery, an anachronism over which towers the starkly modern Marriott at the high-tech Worldgate complex. Wrought-iron fencing and laurel bushes surround the headstone of Laura Ratcliffe Hanna, who once farmed this piece of property and whose early life had been devoted to the Confederate cause.

One can only imagine how many Confederate women "spies" there were—women who would be at home when Union soldiers stopped by, letting slip what they were doing in the neighborhood; women who would dart out the back door as soon as the Yankees left and run for the fields, looking for someone to tell.

Such was the role of Laura Ratcliffe, who warned the "Gray Ghost," Colonel John Mosby, of the host of cavalry hidden in the pines behind the small post he was about to attack. Mosby often used her home as headquarters and would meet with his men at

The last resting place of Confederate sympathizer Laura Ratcliffe Hanna is on her former farm, now the Worldgate complex.

"Mosby's Rock" nearby. The rock also served as a cache for money that Mosby's raiders had stolen from a train.

Although several women spies were loosely associated with Major General J.E.B. Stuart, if only in their imaginations, it was Laura Ratcliffe who inspired his poetry: "And when this page shall meet your glance/Forget not him you met by chance." It was written in an album he gave her, along with his watch chain.

Self-Appointed Chinese Emissary
Prince William County Regional Adult Detention Center
9320 Lee Avenue, Manassas

For 33 years, Larry Wu-Tai Chin worked as a CIA translator while at the same time being under the employ of the Peoples Republic of China. In his briefcase or his clothes, he routinely took agency documents home, where he photographed them with his Minolta.

After he was caught in November 1985, he characterized his activities as a personal peace mission to normalize the U.S. government's relations with China.

How did he ever manage to pass the lie-detector test to work for the CIA? Simple. His questioners asked him everything in English. He found it easier to lie in a foreign language, he said.

He insisted he was a patriot.

But he was also someone addicted to risk-taking. He gambled away most of his take in Las Vegas and Atlantic City. Blackjack was his game.

After the trial, Wu-Tai Chin was faced with the possibility—or impossibility—of two life sentences, plus 83 years. Two weeks after his conviction, on February 21, 1986, he was found dead in his cell at the Prince William County Jail. He had committed suicide by tying a plastic trash bag over his head.

Dueling Defectors
Former safehouse
848 Canal Drive, Great Falls
now a private residence

When James J. Angleton headed
counterintelligence at the CIA, his favorite defector was Anatoliy
Golytsin. Angleton treated him very well, setting him up in a safehouse a few miles from the CIA. In secluded and affluent Great Falls,
it was a lovely gray stone manor house settled back in the natural
camouflage of dense undergrowth. The stone pillars at the drive bore
signs warning off trespassers: "Beware—These premises patrolled by
trained attack dogs." In those days, it was usual to have such signs
at safehouses, which were purchased and used over and over. Now-
adays the agency just rents them short term.

Moles need not apply. In Golytsin, who came out in December
1961, Angleton found a voice that harmonized with his on the
subject of Soviet plots. Soul mates. Both believed that there was a
mole burrowed deeply in the CIA—a secret agent sent by the KGB.
In fact, Golytsin warned that almost every intelligence service in the
world had been penetrated. He also asserted that the Sino-Soviet
split was a ruse to fool the Americans. It was not surprising that on
psychological tests Golytsin was found to be paranoid.

Then another defector arrived on the scene. Yuri Nosenko came
out of the cold in January 1964, a serendipitous time. He accom-
modated the U.S. government with the news that, from the records
he'd seen on Lee Harvey Oswald's trip to the Soviet Union, that
country had had no involvement in the JFK assassination. He also
warned the Americans that their embassy in Moscow was riddled
with bugs, which turned out to be true.It was a deadly game of
dueling defectors. Golytsin said that Nosenko was a disinformation
agent dispatched to clear the Soviets. Furthermore, if Nosenko were
a KGB plant, that meant he was sent to sidetrack Golytsin's leads
on the mole. It just confirmed the mole's existence.

Angleton again relied on his pet defector. While Golytsin had
had the best safehouse in town, Nosenko was held captive by the

132

CIA. For some months he was kept in solitary confinement in an attic room with a single bed and light bulb. Then, his new "prison," in which he was interrogated over a period of two years, was no improvement: Nosenko described it as a "bank vault." In the changing tides of public opinion, Nosenko's raft rose and fell, and rose again. It was remarkable how Nosenko's performance improved on the lie detector test when he was asked nicely. Meanwhile, Golytsin's leads had churned up many suspects but no real spies. Fear of the mole had become more debilitating to the agency than the presence of any actual mole could be.

The ultimate resolution was too hard. In the end, Golytsin and Nosenko were both assumed to be bona fide defectors, and it was left at that. The two defectors have long since retired, reputedly with CIA pensions.

Get Your CIA and KGB Mugs Here
Cassel's Sports and Awards
6655-C Old Dominion Drive, McLean

You can always spot them. "Dark shoes, dark suit, white shirt, bathtub chain hanging around the neck." Kandi Yount, a salesperson at Cassel's Sports and Awards, was describing the store's main clientele—CIA employees. The bathtub chain holds the ID, of course.

"We're their unofficial official store," she said. Cassel's offers beer steins, mugs, hats, T-shirts and sweatshirts in both CIA and KGB vintage, as well as CIA coasters, watches, pens and key rings.

"They come in here and buy eight or ten baseball hats, KGB and CIA, for their baseball teams," Yount said.

The agency considers it inappropriate to sell such souvenirs at the employees' store. Worried that a secret agent might go out on his lawn to pick up the newspaper while wearing his CIA shorts.

There is an ambivalence. During a recent meeting, the agency brought over two busloads of happy shoppers. By contrast, Yount said, "Last summer I saw a bunch of guys come in and I said, 'What you're looking for is in the back.' They didn't like that. One wouldn't even speak to me."

When your customer is the CIA, you just never know. "I'm doing a plaque for them right now," Yount said, "and they can't even give me the name of the guy it's going to."

Chez Espionage
Various McLean restaurants and a French restaurant, somewhere

Once a week, former intelligence officers meet to swap war stories over lunch at a Washington French restaurant codenamed CHEZ ESPIONAGE. There's no point in giving its real name: The group would just move to another restaurant the next week. Hint: It has nothing to do with L'Espionage, a now-defunct restaurant which, in its day, lived up to its moniker.

Anonymously of course, one regular describes the group at Chez Espionage as "just a bunch of hacks who gather to relive and lie. Only there's always someone at the table who checks on you, so you don't get away with the lie." Membership is restricted to "people who used to work together." (You know who you are.) The late David Atlee Phillips, who headed the CIA's Latin America Division and later founded the Association of Former Intelligence Officers, assigned the meeting place its codename. If you should stumble upon the restaurant, the calf's liver is recommended.

For their lunches, current CIA employees may frequent one of the eateries in their neighborhood, such as Charley's Place (6930 Old Dominion Drive), Evans Farm Inn (1696 Chain Bridge Road) and the McLean Family Restaurant (1321 Chain Bridge Road). The spooks who eat there look just like everyone else, only more shifty-eyed. They're likely to be the ones who ask quietly for a corner table where they can't be overheard. Those are the spies. Either that or lovers on an assignation. Could be both.

The nearby Domino's Pizza (1420 Chain Bridge Road) can sometimes get a bead on world crises before most everyone else; they know something's afoot when orders-out burgeon at the CIA.

Inside the Agency
Central Intelligence Agency
Dolley Madison Boulevard, Langley

Try going to the CIA when they're not expecting you, and you will be sternly questioned and asked to leave.

Ah, but if you're on the list! If they have your social security number on the day's appointment roster, that same stern guard dressed like a park ranger will be all boyish smiles. Just inside the gate, which looks a lot like customs, there is a little stopgap measure—a traffic light. If it turns red, people do stop. Otherwise the steel barrier that is poised to rise up from the roadbed will stop their cars for them.

Security is tighter than a briefcase full of documents. But William Kampiles, a CIA watch officer, managed to slip through with the top-secret KH-11 satellite manual tucked under his arm. It was a how-to book on using the satellite's data. The KH-11, known fondly as Big Bird, could make out license plate numbers from its post hundreds of miles up. While appearing to be a dead artificial moon, it relayed its transmissions to another satellite instead of directly to earth, as would have been expected. In 1978, Kampiles sold the manual to the KGB in Athens for $3,000; he's serving time.

Everyone has a fantasy of what the CIA is like—even some employees, who persist in calling headquarters "the campus." No ivy is detectable, however. Driving along the entrance road, one expects to hear a gun shot (target practice, surely) or be startled by guerrilla

135

An aerial view of the CIA clearly shows its two main buildings but does not resolve the license-plate numbers of the cars in the parking lots.

trainees jumping out from the rhododendrons. Truth be known, that sort of training takes place in Camp Peary, near Williamsburg.

One envisions a labyrinth. But the CIA plant is straightforward, at least from the outside, like a candy factory. There are just two main office buildings, one occupied in 1961 and another in 1988, after the agency outgrew the first. Among other lesser buildings on the grounds, a strangely steaming edifice turns out merely to be the power plant. There is The Bubble, also known as the auditorium, and the water tower, which is just a water tower. A modern house mysteriously out of character with the rest of the architecture turns out to be the day-care center. (The children are known by numbers.)

A white clapboard house near the entrance could be a safehouse or a place where they experiment (play with the minds of prisoners, make them think they're at home), or a house destined to be blown up. But it's just where nonagenarian Margaret Scattergood lived—free from fear of burglars—until her death in 1986.

In front of the old building sprawls a long cement overhang, a hotel entrance without a doorman. A multitude of windows on seven floors look out like a million narrowed eyes. Some of them have a green cast—to keep light out, sound in? No one wants to say.

The lobby is full of appropriate symbolism and inspirational messages. On the left is the robust statue of "Wild Bill" Donovan, head of the OSS. No one is seen to genuflect, but it could happen. They used an old belt of his to get the right girth measurement. The statue was delivered recumbent on a pickup truck.

On the right, a bas relief of former director Allen Dulles and, cut into the marble walls, a number of memorial stars that stand for officers who died in the line of duty. Beneath the stars is a book open to a page with dates. Under the dates are the stars for that year and, when possible, the names of the dead corresponding to the stars. Most of the stars have blanks next to them; the names will never be publicly revealed.

The white marble lobby sets a tone of reserved austerity. A serious place. No one gets in without going through one of a battery of special gates, putting in an ID card and punching in a code. Even then the cards don't always work, and sometimes an arm of the gate sticks. The visitor's ID card is unmistakable, with a large orange V and the words "Visitor Escort Required." Everyone wears ID here, all the time.

Inside, one imagines dark empty halls. The cloistered dens of pipesmoking men scheming cosmic agendas into their drifting plumes of smoke. The laboratories of eccentric wild-haired geniuses leaning over their latest fiendish device. And the offices of chilly bureaucrats, immaculately dressed, smooth-faced. If this is a true picture, it is not immediately visible. Most things here are done with computers, anyway.

Actually the halls are light and airy. It's just another government agency—although possibly the employees look wider awake and happier in their work. In some ways, it's no different from other bureaucracies.

The new building's lobby is very different from the old; they had a chance to rethink it. One enters a long corridor under an arched skylight of green-tinted glass. Accents of green marble line the way. Again, the very serious security gate blocks the end of the entrance hall.

A constant reminder of the agency's OSS roots, the statue of "Wild Bill" Donovan stands inside the lobby of the CIA's old building.

Even when you do get past the ID check, there are only a few approved stops for the visitor. Only one of the three cafeterias, for instance. The second is for employees only. The third is for undercover officers. Nobody can eat with them.

Another approved place, in the atrium of the new building, is the Historical Intelligence Collection. Although everything in it is unclassified, of course it is not open to the public. In general, the only tourists who see it are CIA employees on lunch hour.

"There's a fine line between trash and treasure and I cross it every day," says Linda McCarthy, the museum's exhibits coordinator. "Our motto is 'Always say yes.'" About 200 items are exhibited here in the agency's glass-enclosed attic.

On display, "Wild Bill" Donovan artifacts: From his World War I haversack, there are some .45 caliber shells and a Beechnut gum label ("Always Refreshing"). There's the .22 caliber silent and flashless pistol he supposedly fired into a sandbag in the Oval Office to impress FDR with the Research and Development folks. Other things the OSS people made: a "clam" for under a car (if it exploded, the car went with it), and a seismic-intruder detection device (senses movement and looks like dog-do).

Also: the first flag to fly over CIA headquarters; patches for the Bay of Pigs Brigade (never used) and a lantern for the beach (also never used); a handsome ivory-handled cane that quickly converts to a shotgun; a flashlight taken from Ché Guevara when he was captured in Bolivia in 1967; a 300-pound piece of Berlin Wall; Allen Dulles's self-authorized ID card. And so on.

You're not likely to see these things in any other museum. In fact, you're not likely to see them at all.

Christian Renault's Recipes for James Angleton

The former chef of La Niçoise now owns La Petite Auberge in Fredericksburg, Virginia. Here are his recipes for two of Angleton's favorite dishes. When cooking mussels for Angleton, M. Renault made sure to serve him only big ones and to take out any white ones.

Steamed Mussels

Clean the mussel shells with a brush; pull out the beards. Put mussels in a pan with a little bit of white wine, a crushed clove of garlic, some parsley, a good amount of butter and just put them on the stove covered for five minutes and that will steam them open. When they are open there will be a nice broth. Then add a little bit of heavy cream, swirl the pan, put them in a serving dish and send them out. Use Maine mussels.

Spycatcher's Scampi

Buy the big ones, ten shrimp to a pound. Remove the shell and vein. Put a little bit of salt on them. Drag them in flour. Dip into an egg wash, two eggs beaten. Put them into a hot pan with shortening or olive oil. I use shortening; butter burns too fast. Three minutes on top of the stove. Turn the shrimp over in the pan and put into a hot oven for three to four minutes. They're done in seven minutes, opaque but still tender. Take out of the oven and get rid of the grease. Add fresh butter and a garlic clove crushed with a Chinese cleaver. Put in the butter a soupçon of chopped parsley and juice of half a lemon. Swirl in the pan 20 seconds.

Guy Bougère's Poached Salmon for Vitaly Yurchenko

For 16 years, M. Bougère has been chef at Au Pied de Cochon, which never closes.

In a shallow pan, put chopped shallots and butter, white wine and water. Put clean salmon fillet on the top, a little bit of salt and white pepper. Cover with parchment and just bake it. On top of the stove if you want, it's even faster. When it just starts to boil, take it off and let it finish cooking by itself. Serve it with Hollandaise.

Tradecraft from Miss Leslie's New Cookery Book *(1857)*

No stronger methods were required by the Widow Greenhow than food and drink, and her enchanting company. From a popular cookbook, oysters and sherry would have been on her menu for seduction.

Sherry Cobbler

Lay in the bottom of a large tumbler, two table-spoonfuls of powdered loaf sugar, and squeeze over it (through a strainer) the juice of a large lemon that has been softened by rolling under your hand. Then half fill the tumbler with ice, broken very small. Add a large glass of very good sherry wine. Take another tumbler, and pour the liquid back and forward from glass to glass, till completely mixed without stirring. Sip it through a clean straw, or one of the tubes made on purpose.

Roasted Oysters

The old-fashioned way of roasting oysters is to lay them on a hot hearth, and cover them in hot cinders or ashes. When done, their shells will begin to open. The usual way now is to broil them on large gridirons of strong wire. Serve them up in their shells on large dishes, or on trays, at oyster suppers. At every plate lay an oyster knife and a clean coarse towel, and between every two chairs set a bucket to receive the empty shells. The gentlemen generally save the ladies the trouble of opening the oysters, by performing that office for them.

Have on the table, to eat with the oysters, breadrolls, biscuits, butter, and glasses with sticks of celery scraped, and divested of the green leaves at the top. Have also ale or porter.

Advice from
The Virginia House-wife *(1824)*

Belle Boyd and other prisoners often complained about conditions in the Old Capitol Prison. She would likely have owned *The Virginia House-wife,* the most popular cookbook of its era. Published in Washington, D.C., it offered an antidote to noisome vapours.

Vinegar of the Four Thieves

Take lavender, rosemary, sage, wormwood, rue and mint, of each a large handful; put them in a pot of earthen ware, pour on them four quarts of very strong vinegar, cover the pot closely, and put a board on the top; keep it in the hottest sun two weeks, then strain and bottle it, putting in each bottle a clove of garlic. When it has settled in the bottle and become clear, pour it off gently; do this until you get it all free from sediment. The proper time to make it is when the herbs are in full vigour, in June. This vinegar is very refreshing in crowded rooms, in the apartments of the sick, and is peculiarly grateful when sprinkled about the house in damp weather.

What's What in Spydom

Here's an edited version of the FBI's "List of Terminology Used in Foreign Counterintelligence and Counterespionage Investigations."

AGENT—an individual other than an officer, employee or co-opted worker of an intelligence service to whom an intelligence service gives specific assignments. An agent in a target country can be operated by a legal or illegal residency or directly by the center and can be any nationality.

ALIAS—an assumed name, usually consisting of a first and last name, used by an individual for a specific and often temporary purpose.

ASSET—any human or technical resource available to an intelligence or security service for operational purposes.

BACKSTOP—an arrangement made to support a cover story.

BOGIE—a visitor to an official establishment whose identity is not known. See Stray.

BONA FIDES—documents, information, action or codes offered by an individual to establish his good faith, identity, dependability, honesty and motivation.

BRIEFING—preparation of an individual for a specific operation by describing the situation to be encountered, the methods to be employed and the objective; presentation, usually orally, of information.

BRUSH CONTACT—a discreet, usually prearranged momentary contact between intelligence personnel when information or documents are passed. Also known as a brief encounter.

BUILD-UP MATERIAL—see Feed Material.

CACHE—see Dead Drop.

CARBONS—paper that produces secret writing through the use of chemicals.

CENTER—intelligence service headquarters.

CIPHER—a method of concealing the meaning of a message either by replacing its letters or numbers with other letters or numbers in a predetermined manner (a substitution cipher) or by changing the order of the letters or numbers according to certain rules (a transposition cipher).

CIPHER PAD—a small, thin pad of paper sheets printed by machine with a non-repetitive key for use in sending code. Also known as a one-time pad.

CODEWORD—a prearranged word used in communications or conversation to disguise the identity of an individual or object or to convey a meaning other than the conventional meaning.

COMMUNICATIONS INTELLIGENCE (COMINT)—technical and intelligence information obtained from foreign communications.

COMMUNICATIONS SECURITY (COMSEC)—provision of codes and ciphers to any department of the government or military forces requiring them.

COMPARTMENTATION—management of an intelligence service so that information about the personnel, organization or activities of one component is made available to any other component only to the extent required for the performance of assigned duties.

CONCEALMENT DEVICES—innocuous objects designed or adapted as containers for secreting any selected material or equipment. Also called containers.

CO-OPTED WORKER—a national of a country who assists foreign intelligence services. While in most circumstances a co-opted worker is an official of the country, he or she also can be a tourist or student. Sometimes referred to as co-opted agent or co-optee.

COUNTERINTELLIGENCE—actions undertaken to counter the intelligence, espionage and sabotage operations of foreign governments.

COVER—guise used by an individual, organization or installation to prevent discovery of intelligence activities.

COVER STORY—plausible account of background, residences, employment, activities and access furnished to an individual who is operating on behalf of the U.S., to substantiate whatever claims are necessary to successfully carry out an operation. By contrast, a legend is furnished to an illegal or agent by a foreign intelligence service. See Legend.

COVERT ACTIVITIES—activities conducted in a concealed manner that makes it difficult to trace them to the intelligence service or government sponsoring them.

CRYPTOANALYSIS—conversion of encrypted messages to plain text without having knowledge of the key used.

CRYPTOLOGY—the science of secret communications.

CRYPTONYM—codeword or symbol used to conceal operations, organizations, projects and individuals. See Pseudonym.

CULTIVATION—apparently casual but actually deliberate and calculating effort to gain control of an individual, induce him to furnish information and agree to recruitment.

CUTOUT—an individual whose services are used to avoid direct contact between members of an intelligence service.

DEAD DROP—a location where communications, documents or equipment can be left by an individual and picked up by a second individual without any meeting. Also called dead letter box (DLB) or simply drop. Sometimes called a hiding place. A long-term drop is sometimes called a black cache.

DEAD LETTER DROP (DLB)—see Dead Drop.

DEBRRIEFING—a non-hostile interview of an individual who has completed an intelligence assignment or who has knowledge of operational or intelligence significance.

DECEPTION MATERIAL—information passed in any form to an intelligence service or government to mislead. See Disinformation.

DEFECTION—abandonment of loyalty, allegiance, duty or principle to one's country.

DEFECTOR—a national of a country who has escaped from the control of such country or who, being outside such jurisdiction and control, is unwilling to return to that country; he is of special value to another government because he is able to add valuable new or confirmatory information to existing knowledge of his country. In intelligence operations a defector is, in most instances, an official of his country.

DISINFORMATION—carefully orchestrated misinformation prepared by an intelligence service for the purpose of misleading, deluding, disrupting or undermining confidence in individuals, organizations or governments. See Deception Material.

DOCUMENTATION—documents, personal effects, equipment or anything that will lend authenticity supplied to intelligence personnel to support a cover story or legend. See Cover Story and Legend.

DOUBLE AGENT—an agent who is cooperating with a foreign intelligence service on behalf of and under the control of an intelligence service and/or security service of another county.

DRY CLEANING—any technique used to detect surveillance; a usual precaution that intelligence personnel take when actively engaged in an operation.

ELECTRONIC INTELLIGENCE (ELINT)—information derived by intercepting and studying electromagnetic radiation from noncommunication sources, such as radar.

ESPIONAGE—intelligence activity aimed at acquiring classified information from a hostile intelligence service.

FALSE-FLAG RECRUITMENT—occurs when an individual is recruited believing he is cooperating with an intelligence service of a particular country. In fact, he has been deceived and is cooperating with an intelligence service of a different country.

FEED MATERIAL—information that is usually true but unimportant, given to an individual to pass to another intelligence service to maintain or enhance his value to that service. Sometimes called build-up material.

HANDLER—see Principal.

HUMAN INTELLIGENCE (HUMINT)—intelligence collected by observers, informers, agents and the like.

ILLEGAL—an officer or employee of an intelligence service dispatched abroad with no overt connection to the intelligence service that sent him or the government operating the intelligence service. An illegal is operated by the center, not by a legal residency.

INTELLIGENCE COMMUNITY—all components of a government that produce intelligence and counterintelligence.

INTELLIGENCE OFFICER (IO)—a professionally trained member of an intelligence service. He may serve in the home country or abroad, as a member of a legal or illegal residency.

LEGEND—a coherent and plausible account of an individual's background, living arrangements, employment, daily activities and family given by a foreign intelligence service by an illegal or agent. Often the legend will be supported by fraudulent documents. See Cover Story.

LIPPMAN—a special high resolution emulsion used in preparing microdots and mikrats.

MICRODOT—photographic reduction of documents to three by six millimeters. A mikrat is smaller than a microdot.

ONE-TIME PAD (OTP)—see Cipher Pad.

ONE-WAY RADIO LINK (OWRL)—transmission of voice, key or impulses by radio to intelligence personnel who, by prearrangement, can receive and decipher the messages. Also called one-way voice link. See Two-Way Radio Link.

OPEN CODE—seemingly innocuous messages that, by prearrangement, convey a different message.

OVERT ACTIVITIES—activities that may be openly attributed to the government responsible for them.

PICKET SURVEILLANCE—placement of surveillance personnel at locations that encircle an area being watched. Also known as perimeter surveillance.

PERSONA NON GRATA—the official act of declaring a foreign national unwelcome in this country.

POSITIVE INTELLIGENCE—interpreted intelligence.

PRINCIPAL—intelligence officer or co-opted worker directly responsible for the operations of a principal agent or agent. Also known as a handler.

PROVOCATION—activity designed to induce an individual, organization, intelligence service or government to take action damaging to itself.

PSEUDONYM—a false name that looks like a true name. See Cryptonym.

RECOGNITION SIGNALS—prearranged visual signals used by intelligence personnel to identify each other.

RECRUITMENT—the process of enlisting an individual to work for an intelligence or counterintelligence service.

RECRUITMENT IN PLACE—a foreign official who overtly continues to work for his government and covertly provides the U.S. with information of intelligence value.

REDOUBLED AGENT—an agent whose dual role has been discovered by the service on which he is reporting and who is used, wittingly or unwittingly, voluntarily or under duress, to serve the purpose of the latter service against the former service.

RESIDENCY, ILLEGAL—an intelligence establishment in a target country consisting of one or more intelligence officers and possibly one or two other employees with no overt connection to the intelligence service or government that operates it.

RESIDENCY, LEGAL—an intelligence establishment in a target country composed of intelligence officers and employees assigned as overt representatives of their government.

SAFEHOUSE—a location controlled by an intelligence service that provides a secure meeting place for individuals engaged in intelligence operations.

SANITIZE—alteration of information to conceal how, where and from whom it was obtained.

SECRET WRITING (S/W)—invisible writing.

SIGN-OF-LIFE SIGNAL—a signal emitted periodically to signify that an agent is safe.

SIGNAL—a prearranged visual or audio sign that a dead drop has been filled or emptied or that an emergency meeting is needed.

SIGNAL INTELLIGENCE (SIGINT)—intelligence obtained by monitoring foreign radio transmissions from any source including missiles, satellites and spacecraft.

SINGLETON—an illegal who lives in a target country and operates alone, not becoming involved in the operations of agents or illegal residencies.

SLEEPER—an illegal or agent in a foreign country who does not engage in intelligence activities until told to do so.

SOFT FILM—the gelatin emulsion of a film that has been removed from the film base so the film can be rolled or folded and secreted in a small place.

SOURCE—an individual who occasionally furnishes information to foreign intelligence representatives but is not an agent.

SPOTTER—an agent or illegal agent assigned to locate and assess individuals who may be of value to an intelligence service.

STAGING—sending an illegal or illegal agent to another area of the home country or to another country before he is sent to the target country so he can establish a legend and receive training.

STERILIZE—removal of signs that would connect material or devices to an individual, intelligence service or country using them.

STRAY—see Bogie.

SURFACE—public disclosure of an intelligence operation or the identity of intelligence personnel.

TARGET—an individual, organization or intelligence service against which intelligence operations are conducted. Also refers to documents or instruments that an intelligence service is trying to obtain. Also refers to the subject of a surveillance.

TRADECRAFT—specialized techniques used in intelligence operations.

TRIPLE AGENT—an agent who serves three services in an agent capacity but who, like a double agent, wittingly or unwittingly withholds significant information from two services at the instigation of the third service.

TWO-WAY RADIO LINK (TWRL)—transmission of radio messages between intelligence officers and their command centers. See One-Way-Radio Link.

UNWITTING AGENT—an agent who furnishes information without knowing that the ultimate recipient is an intelligence service, or who is unaware of the true identity of the government receiving it.

WALK-IN—an individual who voluntarily offers his services or information to a foreign government.

Books

BAKER, LAFAYETTE C., *History of the United States Secret Service*. (Philadelphia: King & Baird, printers; L.C. Baker, 1867.)

BAMFORD, JAMES, *The Puzzle Palace*. (New York: Penguin Books, 1987.)

BENTLEY, ELIZABETH, *Out of Bondage: KGB Target—Washington, D.C.* (New York: Ivy Books, 1988.)

BESCHLOSS, MICHAEL R., *Mayday: Eisenhower, Khrushchev and the U-2 Affair*. (New York: Harper & Row, 1986.)

BLITZER, WOLF, *Territory of Lies: The Exclusive Story of Jonathan Jay Pollard*. (New York: Harper & Row, 1989.)

BOYD, BELLE, *Belle Boyd in Camp and Prison*. (Cranbury, New Jersey: Thomas Yoseloff, 1968.)

BROWN, ANTHONY CAVE, *The Last Hero: Wild Bill Donovan*. (New York: Vintage Books, 1984.)

BRYAN, GEORGE S., *The Spy in America*. (Philadelphia: Lippincott, 1943.)

BURROWS, WILLIAM E., *Deep Black: Space Espionage and National Security*. (New York: Random House, 1986.)

CAMPBELL, HELEN JONES, *Confederate Courier*. (New York: St. Martin's Press, 1964.)

CARL, LEO D., *International Dictionary of Intelligence*. (McLean, Virginia: International Defense Consultant Services, Inc., 1990.)

CASSIDY, WILLIAM L., *The Official History of the OSS Schools and Training Branch*. (San Francisco: Kingfisher Press, 1983.)

COSTELLO, JOHN, *Mask of Treachery*. (New York: William Morrow and Company, Inc., 1988).

DEMARIS, OVID, *The Director: An Oral Biography of J. Edgar Hoover*. (New York: Harper's Magazine Press, 1975.)

DOBSON, CHRISTOPHER, and RONALD PAYNE, *Who's Who in Espionage*. (New York: St. Martin's Press, 1984.)

FARQUHAR, WILLLIAM HENRY, *Annals of Sandy Spring, or 20 Years' History of a Rural Community in Maryland*. (Cottonport, Louisiana: Polyanthos, 1971.)

GILDERHUS, MARK, *Diplomacy and Revolution*. (Tucson: University of Arizona Press, 1977.)

GREENHOW, ROSE O'NEAL, *My Imprisonment and the First Year of Abolition Rule at Washington*. (London: Richard Bentley, 1863.)

HISS, ALGER, *In the Court of Public Opinion*. (New York: Alfred A. Knopf, 1957.)

KAHN, DAVID, *The Codebreakers: The Story of Secret Writing*. (New York: The MacMillan Company, 1968.)

KANE, HARNETT T., *Spies for the Blue and Gray*. (Garden City, New York: Doubleday & Company, Inc., 1954.)

KESSLER, RONALD, *Escape from the CIA: How the CIA Won and Lost the Most Important KGB Spy Ever to Defect to the U.S.* (New York: Pocket Books, 1991.)

———, *The Spy in the Russian Club.* (New York: Charles Scribner's Sons, 1990.)

———, *Spy Vs. Spy: Stalking Soviet Spies in America.* (New York: Charles Scribner's Sons, 1988.)

LAMPHERE, ROBERT J. and TOM SHACHTMAN, *The FBI-KGB War.* (New York: Random House, 1986.)

LESLIE, ELIZA, *Miss Leslie's New Cookery Book.* (Philadelphia: T.B. Peterson, 1857.)

MARTIN, DAVID C., *Wilderness of Mirrors.* (New York: Harper & Row, 1980.)

MILLER, NATHAN, *Spying for America: The Hidden History of U.S. Intelligence.* (New York: Paragon House, 1989.)

OBERDORFER, DON, "The Playboy Sergeant," in *Great True Spy Stories*, Allen Dulles, editor. (Secaucus, New Jersey: Castle, 1968.)

PAPEN, FRANZ VON, *Memoirs.* (New York: E.P. Dutton and Company, Inc., 1953.)

PINKERTON, ALLAN, *The Spy of the Rebellion.* (Kansas City, Missouri: Kansas City Publishing Company, 1885.)

POWERS, RICHARD GID, *Secrecy and Power: The Life of J. Edgar Hoover.* (New York: The Free Press, 1987.)

RANDOLPH, MARY, *The Virginia House-wife.* (Washington: Davis and Force, 1824.)

RANELAGH, JOHN, *The Agency: The Rise and Decline of the CIA.* (New York: Simon & Schuster, 1987.)

ROSS, ISHBEL, *Rebel Rose: Life of Rose O'Neal Greenhow, Confederate Spy.* (New York: Harper & Brothers, 1954.)

SHEVCHENKO, ARKADY, N., *Breaking With Moscow.* (New York: Alfred A. Knopf, 1985.)

STABLER, HAROLD B., *Some recollections, anecdotes and tales of old times.* (Sandy Spring, Maryland: Harold B. Stabler, 1963.)

STEVENSON, WILLIAM, *A Man Called Intrepid.* (New York and London: Harcourt, Brace, Jovanovich, 1976.)

TIDWELL, WILLIAM A., with **JAMES O. HALL** and **DAVID WINFRED GADDY**, *Come Retribution: The Confederate Secret Service and the Assassination of Lincoln.* (Jackson, Mississippi and London: University Press of Mississippi, 1988.)

TROY, THOMAS F., *Donovan and the CIA.* (Frederick, Maryland: Aletheia Books, 1981.)

U.S. CONGRESS, *Senate Select Committee on Presidential Campaign Activities (Watergate Committee).* (Washington, D.C.: U.S. Government Printing Office, 1973.)

WILKIE, JOHN E., "The Secret Service in the War," in *The American-Spanish War: A History by the War Leaders*. (Norwich, Connecticut: Charles C. Haskell & Son, 1899.)

The War Report of the OSS, Vol. 1, Kermit Roosevelt, editor. (New York: Walker Publishing Company, 1976.)

Watergate: Chronology of a Crisis. (Washington, D.C.: Congressional Quarterly, Inc., 1975.)

The Writings of George Washington from the Original Manuscript Sources, 1745–1799, John Fitzpatrick, editor. (Washington, D.C.: U.S. Government Printing Office, 1932.)

Articles and Unpublished Papers

BALDWIN, ALFRED C., as told to Jack Nelson, "Phone Monitored for Three Weeks," *The Washington Post*, October 6, 1972.

CALLAN, JOHN, "A Spy's Tour of Washington," *Regardie's*, September 1988.

"Downing a Suicide," *The Evening Star*, May 12, 1898.

FISHEL, EDWIN C., "Myths That Never Die," in *International Journal of Intelligence and Counterintelligence*, Vol. 2, No. 1, Spring, 1988.

FRIEDMAN, WILLIAM F., "A Brief History of the Signal Intelligence Service," June 29, 1942, National Archives, Record Group 457, SRH-029.

"Gen. Krivitsky, Former OGPU Leader Who Feared Assassins, Shot to Death in Hotel Here," *The Washington Post*, February 11, 1941.

"Gen. Krivitsky Found Dead; Suicide Finding Questioned," *The New York Times*, February 11, 1941.

KESSLER, PAMELA, "Spy Sites," *The Washington Post*, March 3, 1989.

MARSHALL, ELIOT, "The Blackbird's Wake," *Air & Space*, October/November, 1990.

"On the Roof," National Archives, Record Group 457, SRH-355, part 2.

QUATTLEBAUM, JAMES, "A Spy's Tour of Washington," *Regardie's*, May 1988.

RICHARDS, BILL, "A Defector's High Life Disclosed," *The Washington Post*, October 10, 1978.

RUST, JEANNE, "Portrait of Laura," *Virginia Cavalcade*, Winter 1962-63.

SCHORRECK, HENRY F., "The Telegram that Changed History," National Archives, Record Group 457, SRH-234.

SIMMONS, LINDA J., "The Antonia Ford Mystery," *Northern Virginia Heritage*, Volume VII, No. 3, October, 1985.

WEBER, SANDRA, "Fort Hunt—The Forgotten Story," *The Cultural Resources Management Bulletin*, Vol. 6, No. 3, September 1983.

WILKIE, JOHN E., "Catching Spain's Spies," *The Boston Sunday Herald*, October 2, 1898.

YARDLEY, HERBERT O., "A History of the Code and Cipher Section During the First World War," National Archives, Record Group 457, SRH-030.

Pamela Kessler grew up in Moorestown, New Jersey. In 1963, she came to Washington, D.C., to attend American University, where she majored in English and French. She has lived in the area ever since.

She began her career in journalism at the *Saturday Evening Post* in 1967 and moved on in 1968 to *The Washington Post*. During her 21 years at the *Post*, Kessler worked as a copy editor on the National desk, and as a reporter with feature stories appearing in the Weekend and Style sections.

In 1989, Kessler went on leave from the *Post* to attend the graduate fiction writing program at Johns Hopkins University. She focused on short-story writing, receiving her master's degree. She left the *Post* in 1991 to continue free-lancing: *Undercover Washington*, a work of non-fiction, is her first book.

When she isn't writing, Kessler enjoys ice skating and gardening. She has a son, Mike Whitehead, 25, a guitarist who performs in the Washington area. She is married to Ronald Kessler, a best-selling author specializing in books in the intelligence field, who is also a former *Washington Post* reporter. They live in Potomac, Maryland.